P9-CEY-791

What Your Heart Needs for the Hard Days

Other Books by Holley Gerth

You're Already Amazing

You're Made for a God-Sized Dream

Opening the Door to Your God-Sized Dream

You're Going to Be Okay

The "Do What You Can" Plan (ebook)

If We Could Have Coffee . . . (ebook)

What Your Heart Needs for the Hard Days

52 Encouraging Truths to Hold On To

Holley Gerth

Revell
a division of Baker Publishing Group
Grand Rapids, Michigan

Published by Revell
a division of Baker Publishing Group
P.O. Box 6287, Grand Rapids, MI 49516-6287
www.revellbooks.com

Printed in the United States of America

Library of Congress Cataloging-in-Publication Data is on file at the Library of Congress, Washington, DC.

ISBN 978-0-8007-2288-3

14 15 16 17 18 19 20   7 6 5 4 3 2 1

To My Encouragers

Contents

Introduction

We all have hard days. The kind that make us want to pull the covers back over our heads, move to Hawaii, or eat a dozen cupcakes. Deep inside we know those aren't the best options for our lives or our thighs. So what's a girl to do?

Thankfully, Jesus said we don't "live on bread alone"—that includes cupcakes—"but on every word that comes from the mouth of God" (Matt. 4:4). That means while we may crave all kinds of things, what we really need is truth. We need to know who God is and what he's promised us. We need to remember who we are and have confidence that we're going to be okay. We need to find a way to quiet the hunger pains in our hearts.

The book of Psalms is like a table covered with God's goodness. It's a place I'm often drawn to when I'm feeling down. And it's where we're going to sit together in these pages. So pull up a chair if you're feeling tired, if you're discouraged, or if you just feel a little empty inside.

Because this book has fifty-two entries, you can read it as a daily or weekly devotional. My prayer is that by the end of our time together, you'll walk away with a heart that's full. You'll have more strength, peace, and joy. You'll feel refreshed and nourished in a way that will sustain you through whatever the future may hold.

You're not alone, my friend. We're in this together. Let's "taste and see that the LORD is good" (Ps. 34:8).

XOXO
Holley

1

God Wants to Lift You Up When Life Lets You Down

But you, LORD, are a shield around me,
my glory, the One who lifts my head high.

Psalm 3:3

She stands at the edge of the room and stares at the floor. All around her conversations flow and laughter pours out, yet she feels alone. Another time she might have had the strength to reach out. She might have been able to overcome her insecurity. She might have made the best of this situation. But not today.

Then a voice calls her name. At first she doesn't even respond. But soon she feels a gentle hand on her chin, tilting her face toward the sound of words being spoken to her. She does what she hasn't all day: she looks up. And standing right before her is someone who loves her. Someone who sought her out. Someone who wants to hear about her hard day and her heart. And suddenly she feels a bit different.

We often go through life like the woman standing at the edge of the room. Our hearts are downcast. We don't even have the energy to try anymore. We feel alone. And then Jesus does something that's beyond our comprehension. He comes to us in infinite love and tenderness. *He lifts our heads.*

When we look down, it's usually because we're feeling shame, sadness, or insecurity. Jesus wants to change all of that by reaching out to touch our lives and hearts. When someone lifts up your head, it's an invitation for eye contact. It's a way of clearly showing, "I see you. I'm here with you. I want to connect with you."

Jesus did this over and over again with people during his time on earth. He didn't just casually connect with those around him. He looked into their eyes. He saw their hearts. He met their needs from a place of deep compassion and understanding. Even when a young ruler came asking hard questions, "Jesus looked at him and loved him" (Mark 10:21). He's doing the same with you today. *Jesus is looking at you and loving you.* He's reaching out his hand to cup your chin and lift your face so you can look into his eyes.

What else happens when we lift our heads? Our perspective changes. We may have been staring at the place where we feel stuck and at the difficulties right in front of us. But when we look up, we can see Jesus is in that place with us. We can even dare to look over his shoulder and catch a glimpse of the future he has for us. We know we're going to be okay.

You are not standing at the edge of the room alone today. Right in front of you is a Savior who wants to lift your head and heal your heart. Can you feel his touch and hear his voice? Both are full of love for you. Wherever you are today, he's with you. It's time to look up, my friend.

What My Heart Is Saying to You

Lord, I'm so glad you're here with me today. I choose to believe that's true. Please lift my head and speak to my heart. I trust that you see me, you understand, and you know what I need. I want to share with you . . .

Amen.

What My Heart Is Hearing from You

Psalms 1–3

2

God Makes Sure Even the Darkest Night Leads to Dawn

In peace I will lie down and sleep,
for you alone, Lord,
make me dwell in safety.

Psalm 4:8

"What's going to happen?"

"How will this work out?"

"Do I have the strength to get through this?"

Questions like this swirl inside her mind at the end of a hard day. Her head is on a pillow, but her heart is in another place. One that's filled with fear, anxiety, and uncertainty.

We've all had nights like this one. We stare at the clock as the minutes pass by and sigh, "I used to be able to sleep like a baby." That phrase has always sounded a little odd to me because I have lots of friends with kids, and, well, their babies never seem to sleep as much as the moms and dads would like. But I think that saying comes from what happens when infants do drift off to dreamland in the arms of those who love them. Their little faces are full of peace, and often what would wake many of us doesn't disturb their slumber.

Babies sleep when they know they are secure. They sleep when they're confident their needs will be met. The sleep of a child is an act of trust because they're completely vulnerable—helpless and defenseless.

It's this kind of trust that the psalmist shows when he says, "You alone, LORD, make me dwell in safety." In other words, "I know where my security comes from, and it's from you, God." Like a little child, David knows whose arms will hold him. He knows who will watch over him. He knows he's in the care of One who can be believed.

Hard days can tempt us to place our security where God never intended it to be. We grasp at money, relationships, or even self-reliance to make us feel safe. It's a human response to reach out for what's tangible and what seems like it will give us peace. We try to find a way to stay standing. We want to hold on to what's in front of us with all our might. And yet this verse extends an entirely different invitation than what our minds are screaming at us to do: it invites us to "lie down and sleep" in peace.

In other words, release control. Realize that you can't keep yourself safe. You can't fix this problem. You can't be strong enough on your own. Yes, you can partner with God, but in the same way a baby partners with a parent—in trust, obedience, and surrender. Next time you want to stay up and strive, lie down in peace instead. It's a strange paradox. It's often in the moments when we feel weakest and most vulnerable that God exerts his strength on our behalf.

Lay your head on his chest. Tell him you're afraid and weary. Tell him what you need. Then let your heart rest. You are in God's care, and your security is with him—the One who will never let you go, who can keep you through the darkest night until the dawn.

What My Heart Is Saying to You

Lord, I'm weary and afraid. I need you to comfort me and be my security. Please help me rest in you. Hold me close and fill me with peace in the way only you can. I especially need you to . . .

Amen.

What My Heart Is Hearing from You

Psalms 4–6

3

God Is Thinking about You Today

God will never forget the needy;
the hope of the afflicted will never perish.

Psalm 9:18

The text message pops onto my phone as I sit at a coffee shop. "I'm so sorry! I forgot our meeting today. I'm on my way!"

I smile as I sip my latte. "Let me assure you I'm doing okay," I reply. "And I've certainly done the same thing before. All is well. See you soon."

As humans, we're notoriously forgetful. We can't find the keys. We miss birthdays. We show up late for appointments. It's maddening. Even when something is really important to us, our mind can drop it to make room for what it deems more important. (The system it uses is a complete mystery to me. I can remember an absurd amount of lyrics from eighties music, and yet I can't recall where I put my cell phone a lot of the time.)

Imagine never being able to forget. I mean *never*. Any fact, memory, or bit of relevant information you want is there immediately when you need it. You never overlook a special day, lose a beloved item, or scratch your head while you try to recall the details of a particular event.

That's what reality is like for God. He knows all of eternity in a way we can't even comprehend. His ability to pay attention is unlimited. His recall is perfect. His tender care of us is never compromised by good intentions that don't become reality.

When life gets tough, we can feel as if God has forgotten us. We wonder if perhaps his schedule just got a bit busy. Maybe he placed us where we are and then got distracted by something else. Or it could be that he has some idea of what's going on but the details escape him—after all, he has a lot to manage.

But none of those are true. You serve a God who has the hairs on your head not only numbered but memorized. He knows the details of your life even better than you do. He never loses touch with your heart. And because of that, you can always have hope. Because even if you can't see what God is doing, you can trust he is already acting on your behalf. Nothing is too difficult for him. No challenge is too big. No detail is too small.

The opposite of forgetting is thinking of someone. And God is thinking of you. The God who spoke the world into being, who holds the stars in place, who sent his Son because he loved you so much is thinking of you. Right now. In this moment. In *every* moment.

Pause for a moment and let that reality take hold of your heart. You are not alone. You are not overlooked. You are not forgotten.

You never have been.

You never will be.

You are always on God's mind.

And he is always on your side.

What My Heart Is Saying to You

Lord, sometimes it's hard to know you're there. Thank you for thinking of me, remembering my needs, and working to meet them even when I can't yet see or understand what you're doing. Today I just need to be reassured that . . .

Amen.

What My Heart Is Hearing from You

Psalms 7–9

4

God Will Give You Courage, Not Condemnation

You, Lord, hear the desire of the afflicted;
you encourage them, and you listen
to their cry.

Psalm 10:17

It would be easier to pull the covers back over her head. It would be simpler to let the sun stream through the windows and not rise to greet it. It would be less painful to turn over and let sleep seize her again.

But she doesn't let the depression win. Not today. She pushes back the blankets and puts her feet on the floor. She stretches her arms to the heavens and whispers, "Help me, Jesus." She takes a step away from her comfort zone and into the arms of the Savior who is waiting to walk with her through every moment of her day.

Depression is real. And I believe we are whole beings who need help with every aspect of it—physical, emotional, mental, and spiritual. So if you're struggling with ongoing sadness, then learn the symptoms, go see your doctor, find a wise counselor, and do everything you can to help yourself get what you need.

Also know this: God doesn't condemn you for your feelings. Many of the well-known characters of the Bible struggled with periods of depression too. You're not alone in your struggle, and it's nothing to be ashamed of. I've personally wrestled on and off with depression—and most likely will for the rest of my life. I don't understand why this is a "thorn in my flesh" (2 Cor. 12:7). But thankfully I've learned this truth along the way: God is on my side, especially in those times.

I love that the verse above says that God encourages us. Have you ever thought about that? When the day seems difficult, when you're weary, when you feel like a failure . . . God is encouraging you. For so long I thought of him as standing by and shaking his head as he wondered, "Why can't you get it together?" But that's not his heart toward us at all.

To encourage literally means "to give courage," and that's what God wants to do for us on the hard days. He says to us, "I'm here. I will help you. I will give you strength to take one more step." He looks at your life with infinite love and tenderness. And he knows how hard it is to be us sometimes. He lived in this world. He experienced pain. He died on a cross. Jesus understands how brutal this world can be.

Depression is a hard enough battle on its own. God doesn't want you to add guilt and shame to what you're already trying to overcome. Instead he wants to encourage you.

What if, on the days when it's hard for you to get out of bed, you imagined him reaching out to lift you up instead of being disappointed in you? What if he's cheering as you take your first step into a day that's not one you want to face? What if instead of saying, "Get it together," he's whispering, "Let's do this together"?

That changes everything.

And it can change us.

You are encouraged, not condemned, my friend.

What My Heart Is Saying to You

Lord, I'm so glad you understand firsthand how challenging it can be to live in this world. I'm thankful for the grace and encouragement you extend toward me. I need both and I gratefully receive them. I especially want to say to you today . . .

Amen.

What My Heart Is Hearing from You

Psalms 10–12

5

God Wants to Know, "How Are You, Really?"

How long, Lord? Will you forget me
forever?
How long will you hide your face
from me?
How long must I wrestle with my
thoughts
and day after day have sorrow in
my heart?...
But I trust in your unfailing love;
my heart rejoices in your salvation.
I will sing the Lord's praise,
for he has been good to me.

Psalm 13:1–2, 5–6

She slides into the seat across from me at a busy restaurant. I can see the tiredness in her eyes. She's in a tough season. Many women would have given up by now. But not her. "How are you?" I ask. I really want to know.

"Oh, I'm so blessed!" she responds with a forced smile.

I reach my hand across the table and touch hers. "I mean how are you, really?"

Tears come to the corners of her eyes. "I'm ready to be done with all of this. It's harder than I thought it would be."

So which answer was true? Both.

We're funny as humans. We tend to think in terms of all or nothing. So we insist that life is great when we're breaking apart inside. Because to do otherwise would be to discount all of God's goodness in our lives, right? Not so, friend. We always live with both blessings and brokenness. Challenges and victories. Sorrow and joy. They're all mixed up together.

Acknowledging the hard parts of our lives doesn't mean that we're not grateful for the gifts God has given. We can thank him every day for the child he's given us while also feeling exhausted when that same child gets on our last nerve. We can feel deep appreciation for the job he's provided us with while wanting to beat our heads against our desks in frustration several times a day. We can wonder at how many blessings fill our lives while at the same time sensing an aching emptiness that comes from desires unfulfilled.

God understands both.

So what do we do? We embrace the paradox. We bring our sorrows as well as our joys to God. We say, "Thank you for this job. Please help me, because it's wearing me out." We pray, "Thank you for this child. Please give me strength, because I feel like selling him to the gypsies." We declare, "Thank you for the blessings in my life. Please grant the desire of my heart that feels like a hole in the middle of all this wonderfulness."

What does it tell God when we do that? It says that we trust him. Like the psalmist says above, "I trust in your unfailing love" (v. 5). In other words, "No matter what my circumstances are, I believe that you love me. And I will choose to recognize your love in both the hard and happy parts of my life. I know I'm safe with you and I can bring everything about my experience on this earth to you."

God is leaning toward you right now, and he's asking, "How are you, really?"

He truly wants to know.

And it's okay to tell him.

All of it.

What My Heart Is Saying to You

Lord, it's extraordinary to me that you want to hear what's going on in my life and heart. First, I want to praise you and thank you for how good you are to me. You've blessed me so much! I'm also struggling with some things, so I'm coming to you with a trusting heart to share that . . .

Amen.

What My Heart Is Hearing from You

Psalms 13–15

6

God Says You're a Delight, Not a Disappointment

The Lord was my support.
He brought me out into a spacious place;
he rescued me because he delighted
in me.

Psalm 18:18–19

A friend encounters an unexpected crisis. Our little circle makes plans to provide meals, meet practical needs, step in and do what we can. We're there to offer support. And every time I watch this happen, it's like a miracle to me.

What's an even greater miracle is that God does the same for us. When something difficult happens, it's easy to wonder, "Where are you, God?" And his answer is always the same: "I'm with you." Sometimes he makes his presence known through the hands and feet of people in our lives. Sometimes he quietly whispers to our hearts. Sometimes he works through circumstances to let us know we're not alone.

Why does God do this? The answer in the psalm above seems downright scandalous. David says, "He rescued me because he delighted in me." Yet when bad things happen in our lives, one of the first assumptions we often make is that God must be really upset with us.

David certainly could have believed that to be true. When he wrote the words above, he'd spent years running from King Saul. It would have been easy for David to assume, "I must have heard God wrong. He doesn't want me to be king after all. If he did, the current king wouldn't be trying to knock me off." Instead David steadfastly holds to the belief that God loves, supports, and even delights in him. He trusts that even in this challenging circumstance, God is acting on his behalf.

What assumptions have your circumstances led you to make about how God feels about you? Are those really true?

The enemy would love to persuade you that God is against you. He would love for you to become convinced that you don't have God's support. He would love to make you believe that you've fallen beyond God's ability to hold you up.

Will you pause for a moment and reject those lies? We live in a fallen, broken world, and we all face difficulties. That doesn't mean we're being punished. Jesus lived an absolutely perfect life, and yet he was still "a man of suffering, and familiar with pain" (Isa. 53:3). None of us gets to go through life without hard times. That doesn't say anything about you except this: you're human.

God knows that as humans we're weak and frail. He knows we need help. He wants to offer that to us. Yet it's up to us to receive it. And if we think he's mad at us, then that's a lot harder to do.

Perhaps it's time to shift your perspective to align with what's really true.

God isn't disappointed in you.

He's delighted with you.

And he will give you the support you need.

What My Heart Is Saying to You

Lord, thank you so much for supporting and rescuing me. Because of the challenges I'm facing, it's tempting to believe you're mad at me or that I'm a disappointment to you. Help me to believe you delight in me and your love for me is secure forever. I'm trusting that you . . .

Amen.

What My Heart Is Hearing from You

Psalms 16–18

7

God Will Help You Stand Tall through It All

Some trust in chariots and some in
horses,
but we trust in the name of the L*ORD*
our God.
They are brought to their knees and fall,
but we rise up and stand firm.

Psalm 20:7–8

"How are you doing this week?" I ask in an email that makes its way to her inbox. She replies a little later, "Feeling a little low." It's interesting how we use the word "low" to describe challenging times in our lives. When life brings hard times, it's difficult to look up and stand tall.

Yet in the verses above, David seems to view being "low" as a place where God can work. He first describes those who trust in chariots and horses—those who are riding high through life. He sees their lofty position can't last. Eventually, what they've placed their confidence in will fail. And when it does, they'll fall. In contrast, he says that when we begin on our knees, then we're in a position for God to take hold of us, raise us up, and make us stand firm.

The temptation can become to stay down even after God has said it's time to rise up. We can have false beliefs that tell us this life is all about difficulties, so we're not allowed to stand tall. So we go through our days bent down in insecurity and discouragement when God never intends for us to do so. Over and over in Scripture, being "low" is meant to be a temporary situation:

> He lifted me out of the slimy pit,
> out of the mud and mire;
> he set my feet on a rock
> and gave me a firm place to stand.
> (Ps. 40:2)

> In his love and mercy he redeemed them;
> he lifted them up. (Isa. 63:9)

> Humble yourselves before the Lord, and he will lift you up. (James 4:10)

Yes, we will all have times when life knocks us down. That's simply part of being human. Yet God doesn't want us to stay there forever. So what do you do if you find yourself in that place? Fight to get back on your feet. Do whatever it takes: ask God for help, reach out to friends, see a doctor, join a support group, take care of yourself.

Make a list of every area of your life—spiritual, physical, emotional, mental, and social. In each one choose a small, simple thing you can do to help in your situation. If it takes five minutes or less, even better. What matters most is not the immediate outcome, because you may be in for a long journey. What matters is that you've made a decision to get back on your feet again. You have said, "I know life is hard, and sometimes I'm going to end up being down, but I'm not going to stay here forever."

I'm not talking about plastering a smile on your face and pretending everything is okay when it's not. That's not helpful either. I actually mean the opposite—that it's time to get really honest about how hard things are as well as the help you need. God wants to be your partner in these circumstances. Through his gentleness, love, and patient timing, he wants to lift you up and give you a new, stronger place to stand.

What My Heart Is Saying to You

Lord, I'm feeling low and a bit discouraged. I'm on my knees and I'm asking you to please take me by the hand and raise me up. Please show me how to be part of the process too. Give me courage to ask for help in whatever way I need. I love you and I believe you're going to . . .

Amen.

What My Heart Is Hearing from You

Psalms 19–21

8

God Will Give You Everything You Need

The LORD is my shepherd, I lack nothing.
He makes me lie down in green
pastures,
he leads me beside quiet waters,
he refreshes my soul.

Psalm 23:1–3

The women sit in a circle around the table. Some are young moms who have just dropped their children off in the nursery. Others are retired grandmas who have transitioned to a new season. Every age and stage of life is represented. Together we're getting ready to begin a weekly study. Before we start, the leader says, "Let's go around the group and everyone share how they're feeling this morning in one word." The universal answer: *tired*.

That happened years ago, and yet I still often think of the answer those women gave that morning. I remember it when I get together with a group of friends and we talk about our busy schedules. I recall it when I look at social media updates. I ponder it when I watch TV and see the hectic pace our world asks us to keep.

We are tired. And when life brings challenges, the little bit of margin we may have is quickly taken up. We find ourselves weary and then wonder why it's so hard to enjoy our lives. In other words, we're sheep in need of a shepherd.

I heard once that sheep have to be made to lie down. And that they only do so when they feel secure. Apparently a sheep is capable of wearing itself out. It needs someone to say, "Take a break, buddy." We're not so different. And Jesus knows that's true about us. That's why he says that he will be our shepherd. He will make sure that we lack nothing . . . including rest.

I love how the verse above says that the shepherd has the sheep lie down in "green pastures." What does a green pasture mean to a sheep? It means its needs are going to be met. The sheep is not worrying about going hungry. God wants us to live that way too. And not just when it comes to our physical needs but also those in our hearts as well. He says, "Lie down, daughter. I'm going to take care of your needs. You can stop striving. Rest."

He also leads us to "quiet waters." Sheep need water that's quiet in order to be able to quench their thirst. They don't want to drink from raging rivers or stand on shores with crashing waves. We also need still places to be refreshed. Our schedules may feel like a tsunami is coming toward us, yet our Shepherd says that he has "quiet waters" for us to drink from instead.

Our role in all of this is to choose to be led by our Shepherd and not by our society. If sheep followed other sheep, they'd soon get in trouble. The flock would be worn out, in danger, and deprived of what it needed to survive. When we let the world around us define our need for rest, we put our hearts at risk. You have a good Shepherd. He doesn't want to drive you so hard that you fall down from exhaustion. He doesn't want to force you to go through life without nourishment and refreshment. If you're exhausted and you feel like you're just "doing what you have to do," then it's time to pause and see whose lead you're following.

A full schedule and an empty heart is a sure sign that it's time to draw closer to the Shepherd again. He's promised that you will lack nothing. What are you holding on to out of fear? What is not bringing real nourishment in your life? Where do you need to stop striving and instead begin trusting again?

Our Shepherd knows this about sheep: they're prone to stray. They don't even mean to do so a lot of the time. They get distracted by what looks good and can end up taking a long walk that wears them out. If that's happened to you, it's okay to ask the Shepherd to come get you and bring you home. Tell him your heart is hungry and thirsty. Tell him you need to lie down (yes, go take a nap!). Tell him your soul needs to be restored. You're not going to be in trouble. Shepherds understand sheep. Yours already knows where you are and what you've been through, and it brings him joy to care for you.

What My Heart Is Saying to You

Lord, I'm so grateful I belong to a good and faithful Shepherd like you. Thank you for watching over me and caring for all my needs. You understand me even better than I understand myself. Today I'm coming to you and asking for . . .

Amen.

What My Heart Is Hearing from You

Psalms 22–24

9

God Will Never Reject You

Do not reject me or forsake me,
God my Savior.
Though my father and mother forsake me,
the Lord will receive me.

Psalm 27:9–10

She looks at the phone ringing in her hand but doesn't answer. She tells herself she'll call back when she feels better. She turns down the invitation to a party that weekend. What could she add to a get-together right now? She decides to let the couch be her closest friend for just one more day.

It doesn't ask for anything, and its open arms are always ready to receive her.

Withdrawing from those around us is one of the surest signs we're hurting. I'm especially drawn to this tactic. Even though I love being with people, it takes a lot of energy for me. And when I'm feeling down, it sometimes seems like that energy is just not there. I hesitate to start a conversation, show up, or connect because I feel like I won't have anything to offer. I tell myself that I'll get it together and then I'll let people back into my life.

But that's not the way God created us to live. Listen, my friend: we don't heal alone. It's just not the way God has made the world to work. We need each other for encouragement, strength, and support. So if you feel like hiding today, can I gently whisper that it might be a sign that what you really need most is to show your hurt to another human being?

Certain lies come into our minds that make it harder to reach out. First, the enemy tries to tell us that we have nothing to give and so we should simply stay away. But Jesus said it's "more blessed to give than to receive" (Acts 20:35). When we don't let others meet our needs, we cheat them out of the greater blessing of giving to us.

We also hear the lie that if we're weak or broken, we're not acceptable. Surely we'll be rejected. Yet the truth is, none of us are perfect. We're all messy. We're all in process. We're all still trying to figure life out. If we wait until we *get it together* to be with others, then we won't *be together* with anyone ever again.

So what can give us the courage to move past these lies and back into love? The passage above gives us the reassurance we need. God says, "No matter what other people do, I will not reject you. I will always receive you. I will never leave you." Sometimes people will say the wrong thing. Sometimes they won't be there for you. Sometimes they'll let you down. And we can handle that when we know that God won't ever do any of those things to us. That truth frees us up to love and be loved by people without leaning on them in ways no one can withstand.

And the God who lives within you lives in other believers too. That means he can help them love you. God wants to use other people in our lives to bring us comfort, joy, friendship, wisdom, or whatever else we might need. In order for that to happen, we have to be willing to open our hearts and receive. Love is always risky. There's simply no way around that reality. Having confidence in God's perfect care makes us brave enough to reach out. Even if we don't get the response we want, we can trust God will always give us the love we need.

What My Heart Is Saying to You

Lord, you know firsthand how challenging it can be to connect with people sometimes. Yet you choose to love anyway. Help me to do the same. When I want to withdraw, please give me the courage to connect. I believe you will provide the people we need for every season of our lives. Right now I especially need someone who . . .

Amen.

What My Heart Is Hearing from You

Psalms 25–27

10

God Wants to Update Your Wardrobe

You turned my wailing into dancing;
you removed my sackcloth and
clothed me with joy,
that my heart may sing your praises
and not be silent.
Lord my God, I will praise you forever.

Psalm 30:11–12

When she first starts coming to see me for counseling, all she wears is black. Occasionally a gray sweater or scarf makes its way into her wardrobe. But overall her dark clothes reflect the way her heart feels. She looks lovely in those colors, but I long for the day when she'll be ready to wear a blue to match her sparkling eyes or a red that reflects her smile. It takes a while, but that moment comes. And when she sits down on my couch one day in sunny yellow, I know we're almost done.

What we wear on the outside often reflects how we feel on the inside more than we realize. In our culture, that choice is often subconscious. We go through a difficult time and eventually realize our closets have become filled with darker hues. "Huh," we think. "I didn't realize that I was picking those colors all the time."

In the psalmist's culture, the connection between outward dress and inward distress was more direct. When someone mourned in ancient Israel, they put on sackcloth to show the world that they had experienced loss. Sackcloth was a coarse cloth similar to burlap. It rubbed against the skin and showed the world, "Life is rough right now." I imagine when people saw sackcloth, it helped them instantly empathize with the one wearing it because they'd worn it at certain times in their lives too.

If you saw someone in sackcloth, your first instinct would probably be to try to get them to take it off so they'd be more comfortable. But of course that would only be a partial solution. Otherwise you'd leave your friend standing naked in the street, and that would lead to a whole new kind of trauma. Sackcloth needs not just to be removed but also to be replaced.

The same is true of our heartache. When we see someone who has suffered a significant loss, we can often simply try to make that person stop hurting. That can lead us to say insensitive things like, "This must be for the best" or "You'll see them again one day." While we mean well, comments like those are like stripping off someone's sackcloth. Instead of helping, we leave their hearts even more exposed. What our hearts need is something new to cover them in hard times. And that's what God offers.

The psalmist says God "removed my sackcloth and clothed me with joy." God wants to exchange our pain for joy. He wants to give us something better for our hearts to wear. Does that happen all at once? No, because grief is the way he has created for us to process life. Grief can feel like a negative emotion, but it's actually a positive one because it moves us forward over time. Grief covers our hearts for a season until we're ready for joy again.

Our role is to be sensitive to ourselves and each other so we can understand the timing for our wardrobe switch. If we try to make ourselves stop hurting before we've finished healing, then we go through life with hearts that are bare and vulnerable. It takes time to be ready for joy again, and we need to be patient. Give yourself permission to hurt. It's okay. And you can have hope even in those times because you know that you will one day be clothed with joy again.

And what happens when joy covers us again? We praise the One who has brought it to us in a way and time that fits our lives just right.

What My Heart Is Saying to You

Lord, thank you for not only helping me heal but also replacing my hurt with something better. I appreciate your patience and tenderness as I'm learning to live in joy again. One part of my heart that feels even more vulnerable and exposed than the rest today is . . .

Amen.

What My Heart Is Hearing from You

Psalms 28–30

11

God Is Saying Good Things about You

In the shelter of your presence you hide
them
from all human intrigues;
you keep them safe in your dwelling
from accusing tongues.

Psalm 31:20

The news has hit her hard. He's leaving. The decision makes her question everything—her hair, her heart, her life. She wonders aloud what questions other people will ask too. "I know people are going to talk," she says, "and I'm scared of what they'll say." I nod as I recall hurtful words from painful places in my own past. Sometimes people wound us with words just when we need encouragement most.

Thankfully, Jesus understands what that's like. During his time on earth he experienced criticism, misunderstanding, and unsupportive words from those he depended on most. "Sticks and stones can break my bones but words will never hurt me" did not come from the pages of Scripture! The God who spoke the world into being knows that words can have an impact.

That's exactly why he promises to keep our hearts safe—no matter what anyone says. He hides us from "human intrigues." In other words, the nosy questions, the gossip, the misunderstandings. And where he hides us is truly beautiful. He hides us "in his presence."

Those words bring to mind a little girl running to her mama for comfort after being teased at school. The mom bends down and her daughter buries her face in the chest of one who loves her. The taunts of the girls fade away and all she can hear is her mother's heartbeat.

Imagine if the bullies came toward that mom and daughter. You can bet mama would be raising a hand that clearly says, "Stop right there. You're not messing with my girl. Don't you say another word."

When the accuser of our hearts comes at us, Jesus does the same. He speaks on our behalf. No matter what anyone may say, Jesus is talking truth about you today. "Who then is the one who condemns? No one. Christ Jesus who died—more than that, who was raised to life—is at the right hand of God and is also interceding for us" (Rom. 8:34).

Jesus is saying . . .

You are loved (see 1 John 4:16–18).

You are accepted (see Rom. 15:7).

You are chosen (see 1 Pet. 2:9).

You are *his*.

What he says about you is the ultimate truth. And he always gets the final word.

What My Heart Is Saying to You

Lord, I'm human and it's hard for me not to listen to what other people say. Please protect me from words that could hurt me and replace them with your truth instead. I need to hear your voice whisper to my heart today . . .

Amen.

What My Heart Is Hearing from You

Psalms 31–33

12

God Enjoys Your Joy

The Lord be exalted,
who delights in the well-being of his
servant.

Psalm 35:27

She stands with a baby on her hip. This morning her son is all smiles. She kisses the top of his head and says, "I'm so glad we figured out how to stop him from getting ear infections. He's so much happier now!" As if to comply, her little one offers an extra giggle at that moment. I know that my friend has endured many sleepless nights throughout this process, and I continue to be amazed at her love. "You're a wonderful mama," I tell her.

Parents naturally want their children to thrive (unless something like severe mental illness or a drug addiction prevents them from doing so). Moms feel distress when a baby can't be consoled or comes down with a cold. And they delight when their little ones are healthy and strong. We would all agree a mom is supposed to "delight in the well-being of her child."

Yet we sometimes wonder if God is the same way. The first time I read Psalm 35:27, I thought my Bible had a typo. I'd been raised in a denomination that placed a heavy emphasis on rules and suffering. From what I could tell, God didn't seem very committed to my happiness. Yet through the years I've come to understand that my joy brings my heavenly Father joy too.

That doesn't mean we get everything we want. At lunch with my friend a few weeks later, her adorable boy decided a bug from the corner might make a nice appetizer. Of course she quickly took it away and washed his hands. Did he respond with glee? No, ma'am. He hollered like she was the meanest mama ever. At that moment, he didn't believe she was acting on behalf of his well-being. He wanted that bug and didn't understand why he couldn't have it.

What about the times when it's not a bug we want but something really good? God is raising his children in an imperfect world too. And even though he would like to spare us from all pain, the broken place we live in makes that impossible for now. But he has promised to one day take us to heaven where there will be no more tears, our questions will be answered, and all we long for most will be given to us. In the meantime, faith requires a lot of trust in the ultimate goodness of our Father.

That's why it's essential for us to believe God is committed to our well-being. If we believe "God is a killjoy who isn't really interested in my joy or happiness," then we'll believe hard times are punishment from him. But if we know his heart is to bring what's best to his children, it changes everything. Then we can say, "God delights in my well-being, and even if things aren't okay now, I can trust him to make them better."

We will go through difficulties in this life. We will face challenges. We will have questions that don't get answered until heaven. But we can know that even in all that, God wants us to thrive. He delights in seeing us enjoy our lives. He wants what's best for us. What kind of father would he be if he didn't?

This also means it's okay to take care of yourself when you're going through something tough. Make a list of what refills you and make time for it. Take a walk outside. Watch a movie that makes you laugh out loud. Have coffee and a treat with a friend. Those are gifts from a good and gracious God who knows it's hard to be in this world. As author Gary Thomas says in *Pure Pleasure*:

> Spiritual triumph begins and ends with finding our satisfaction in God above all things. We serve a generous God, however, who eagerly wants to bless us with many other pleasures, gifts from his hand, that delight us—and in delighting us, bring pleasure back to him. Rather than seeing these gifts as competitors that steal our hearts from God, perhaps we can gratefully receive them. . . . When we acknowledge these pleasures, we acknowledge God as a genius creator of brilliant inventions.[1]

We also acknowledge him as a faithful and kind heavenly Father who loves to find big and small ways to bring joy to his children—especially on the hard days.

What My Heart Is Saying to You

Lord, thank you for being a loving heavenly Father who delights in the well-being of his children. Your kindness and goodness show in everything you do. Even in the toughest times, you want to bring us joy. You've helped me today by . . .

Amen.

What My Heart Is Hearing from You

Psalms 34–36

13

God Won't Let You Fall

The Lord makes firm the steps
of the one who delights in him;
though he may stumble, he will not fall,
for the Lord upholds him with his
hand.

Psalm 37:23–24

The ice had spread across the sidewalk in a thin layer. I tried to be brave and navigate the few steps to my driveway. I should have known better. It only took a moment for me to lose my balance. I pictured the neighbors snickering from behind their windows as I gracefully smacked my bottom on the concrete. I called for my husband, and he quickly came to my rescue. Step-by-step we made our way down to the mailbox together. As soon as I slipped, a strong hand under my elbow held me up.

That's essentially what changes when we begin to walk with Jesus. Life is still precarious. We'll have slick situations and challenging circumstances to navigate. But even when we feel a bit unsteady, we no longer have to worry about falling. Someone bigger and stronger than we are is right by our side to keep us standing.

Emotionally we may *feel* as if we've fallen. But there's a difference—we still have solid ground to place our feet on even then. What is that solid ground? It's the truth of who we are and what God promises no matter what. We can stand firm on these truths:

> God has a plan and purpose for our lives (see Prov. 19:21).
>
> He has our best interest in mind even when it's hard to see (see Rom. 8:28).
>
> We're going to make it through this no matter what happens (see Isa. 43:2).

Here's the catch: we can still choose to act like I did when I first went out the door on that icy day. Even though I'm clumsy enough to run into my own coffee table, I thought, "It's just ice. No big deal." In other words, I approached my circumstances with pride. Since I can't be an example in this case, let me be a warning. It's much wiser to acknowledge that yes, we do need to lean on the arm of someone who loves us. We require help. We can't make it on our own.

When we say that to Jesus, he's not disappointed in us. He's delighted to walk by our side. That's why he came—to be with us. And he's still willing to be with us every step. All we have to do is ask. We don't have to wait until we're facing trouble to do so. "Black ice" can be invisible until you're right on top of it. Even when the surface of our future seems smooth, there can be more ahead than we think. Only Jesus knows where the slick spots are and how we can make it through them.

The best time to ask for help is before our footsteps falter. But even if we find ourselves in the middle of an unexpected challenge, it's never too late. Jesus is always ready and willing to hold us up when we start to stumble.

What My Heart Is Saying to You

Lord, life can be more challenging than it seems on the surface. When I begin to slip, please hold me up. An area where I especially need your support today is . . .

Amen.

What My Heart Is Hearing from You

Psalms 37–39

14

God Is Working on Your Behalf

Many, Lord my God,
are the wonders you have done,
the things you planned for us.
None can compare with you;
were I to speak and tell of your deeds,
they would be too many to declare.

Psalm 40:5

Her birthday comes closer, and over coffee she confides her fears. "I know it's really just another day," she says, "but for me it's a whole new decade! What if everyone forgets?" I nod sympathetically and try to stifle a smile as I think of the surprise party invitation that came in my mailbox that day. "Everyone loves you," I reply. "You know that, right?" She answers with a grin, "Yes, I know. But a little proof sure helps!" We laugh together at how true that is sometimes.

A couple of weeks later when my friend walks through the door, shouts of "Surprise!" greet her ears. "You guys!" she exclaims. "You've been working on this all along, and I didn't know it?" We gleefully tell her of conversations and plans unfolding while she was totally unaware. While she'd been worrying, we'd been working.

We're human, and it's natural for us to want to *see* to believe. We can wish prayer were more like talking to a genie in a bottle. Say a few words and *poof*—the answer appears. Or we can long for God to send us an itinerary of his plans for our lives. At least a status update would be nice. But often when it seems we need proof of his love the most, it can be hardest to find.

So what's God doing in those times? Where is he? He's busy working on our behalf. He's promised to work all things together for good, and we can rest in that even when we don't see the results yet. Is that fun? Um, no. Like my friend, when we can see an important day or difficult circumstance coming, fear tries to tell us that we're going to be alone, overlooked, forgotten.

But God declares, "I will not forget you" (Isa. 44:21)! He will not forget your birthday. He will not forget your troubles. He will not forget the details of your life. And not only will he not forget, but he is actively working out a solution for what you need. Will it be what you expected? Probably not. God seems to yell, "Surprise!" fairly often in our lives too. Will it be exactly what you want? Not likely. But because God loves you, it will be best.

So what do we do while God is working? First, we can tell him what we need. "Do not be anxious about anything, but in every situation, by prayer and petition, with thanksgiving, present your requests to God" (Phil. 4:6). This isn't about filling God in, because he already knows. Instead it's about filling us with peace. "And the peace of God, which transcends all understanding, will guard your hearts and your minds in Christ Jesus" (Phil. 4:7).

Then we can choose to actively wait on God. "But those who hope in the LORD will renew their strength. They will soar on wings like eagles; they will run and not grow weary, they will walk and not be faint" (Isa. 40:31). Waiting on God is not passive. As you can see, he may ask you to soar, run, and walk with him in the process. What matters is that in all those things your heart is still at rest because you know that ultimately God is the one doing the work.

And when God finally does show us what he's been up to, we show our gratitude. We can tell him, "Thank you for planning all this for me. Thank you for working behind the scenes. Thank you for bringing this together in your perfect timing." You might even add, as my friend did on the day of her surprise party, "I felt loved before, and now I do even more."

What My Heart Is Saying to You

Lord, sometimes it's hard to wait to see what you're doing in my life. The human part of me wants so much to understand it all right now. Please fill me with peace and show me what to do in this season. A request I'd like to bring you today is . . .

Amen.

What My Heart Is Hearing from You

Psalms 40–42

15

God Doesn't Want You to Try So Hard

It was not by their sword that they won
the land,
nor did their arm bring them victory;
it was your right hand, your arm,
and the light of your face, for you
loved them.

Psalm 44:3

She lists the different things she's tried:

"I've read books."

"I've gone to conferences."

"I've been to counseling."

She goes on to say that in spite of all her efforts, nothing has changed in her life. I look at her, hoping my compassion for her weariness will come through in my words. "You don't have to try so hard."

She looks up, and a tear streams down her cheek. "I don't?" she asks as she sniffs into a tissue. "But isn't this what God expects?" I shake my head and reassure her that her life really can be less about trying hard and more about trust.

Of course, all of the things she listed above can be helpful tools. I wouldn't be writing books if I didn't think they could benefit women. But even the best things in our lives can become "swords" like the psalmist describes above. In other words, we can start believing the tools others have used guarantee instant victory for us too.

Then it becomes tempting to rely on our own strength (our "arm") to achieve that victory for our lives. We think if we just do enough, then things have to get better. It can start to feel as if everything is depending on us. Those "swords" we thought would be so helpful can suddenly seem like a lot to keep holding up.

When we start resorting to our swords and our strength, it usually simply means this: we're afraid.

We don't know what to do, so we decide the safest strategy is simply to do *more*. Doing so at least gives us a sense of control. Yet over time we realize not only are our circumstances not changing, we're flat-out exhausted.

It's often in that moment that we're ready for God to come to our aid. That's when we need his "right arm, hand, and the light of his face." What does he do with those? I believe it looks different in each circumstance. But often it seems that he uses his arm to beckon us to him. His hand takes the sword from ours, and he says, "You can lay that down, daughter. You don't have to fight anymore." Then he looks us in the eyes and reassures us, "I love you. I'm going to take care of you. It's time to stop trying so hard and instead trust me."

You don't have to try so hard.

Really.

Can you lay down your sword and let your tired heart rest in that today?

What My Heart Is Saying to You

Lord, it's easy to try really hard to make everything right in my life—especially when I feel afraid. Today I'm slowing down, taking a deep breath, and coming to you for victory in this area . . .

Amen.

What My Heart Is Hearing from You

Psalms 43–45

16

God Is within You So You'll Never Be without Him

God is within her, she will not fall;
God will help her at break of day.

Psalm 46:5

The headlines stream across the bottom of the television: The weather is wreaking havoc through flooding in the South. Threats of terrorism have rattled confidence in the East. A criminal on the loose has people locking their doors tight in the North. And a virus outbreak is packing hospitals in the West. In every direction, chaos and crises seem to threaten our lives. I click the Off button on the remote and consider looking for monsters under the bed. Instead I close my eyes and ask God, "Where is peace possible in this world?" It seems the answer comes, "Within you, because that's where I am."

When we look at what's around us, it's easy to be overwhelmed. In the days of ancient Israel, a wall guarded the city of Jerusalem. It could easily seem as if that wall kept the people safe. Yet God told his people, "It's not about what's around you. It's about who is within you." They lost sight of this reality. They put their trust in their own strength and refused to rely on God. And when they did, Jerusalem fell and the people were exiled. No wall could be strong enough without God's protection.

We build walls in our lives too. We think, "If I can just save enough money for retirement, then I'll be secure." We tell ourselves, "If I can just stay in shape, then my confidence will be unshakable." Or "If I can have a husband and children who love me, they'll be my protection." All of those can be wonderful blessings and part of God's provision in our lives, but when hard times come, those things won't be able to keep us from being overrun by the enemy.

Jesus said, "Seek first his kingdom and his righteousness, and all these things will be given to you as well" (Matt. 6:33). He didn't say to ignore every aspect of your life except the spiritual. Jesus knows we're in the physical world and we have responsibilities to take care of here. That can be part of seeking his kingdom too, through the guidance of the Holy Spirit. We do need to save for retirement. It's wise to see the doctor if the flu is going around and we don't feel well. It's okay to install alarm systems in our homes. Those just aren't supposed to be what ultimately gives us a sense of security in this fallen world.

We tend to focus on the external, especially in times of trouble. What God is encouraging us to do is focus on the internal and eternal instead. Start with your heart first. Make sure God is on the throne there. Deal with any areas of rebellion in your life. Build your inner strength and trust in him intentionally each day.

God has not promised you safety. But he has promised you security. Nothing can overcome you because nothing is too big for him. That means there's no breaking news that can break you, my friend.

What My Heart Is Saying to You

Lord, I pray that you will be my ultimate security. When I'm tempted to place my trust in something or someone else, help me to rely on you instead. Thank you for promising that as I seek you first, you will give me everything else I need, including . . .

Amen.

What My Heart Is Hearing from You

Psalms 46–48

17

God Is Speaking to You Today

Our God comes
and will not be silent.

Psalm 50:3

The tears silently slip from my eyes in the quiet of my bedroom. I wipe them away with frustrated fingers. It's Mother's Day. For years my husband and I tried to have children. Over a very long, twisty-turny process, God brought us to a place where we knew we were called to be parents in a different way. My heart healed. And yet sometimes the scars from that season still ache like an old injury on a rainy day.

I didn't want to feel sad again this Mother's Day. I didn't want to cry. Most of all, I didn't want to feel out of control. Where was God? He'd brought me here, and yet I struggled to sense his presence in this moment.

When I'm hurting, I often try to lose myself in words. So I grabbed a book from the shelf. It had been sitting there for months, but I had neglected to open it yet. I began to read *Bittersweet* by Shauna Niequist. I made it about halfway through and felt ready to drift to sleep, but I felt compelled to turn the page to just one more chapter. And when I did, these are the words that greeted me:

> *Happy Mother's Day*
>
> I have been mothered by a whole tribe of women, some who had children of their own, and some who didn't. I thank God for each of them, and thank them for mothering me when I needed it, and for giving me such a rich variety of images for what it means to be a mother. Mother's Day is about looking through our lives and recognizing the act of mothering everywhere we see it, and more than that, recognizing that when any

> of us mother—when we listen, nurture, nourish, protect—we're doing sacred work.[1]

Shauna had also been through a miscarriage, and she wrote from a place of knowing, understanding, speaking to the pain I felt. Then my dear friend Cathy sent me a text that said, "Thinking of you, my friend, and all the women you have impacted. I am a better mother because of you. I will continue to pray for you that God would give you the desire of your heart. I know you would be an awesome mommy. But I also know that God can use you in so many ways to touch lives that he couldn't if you were consumed with a baby."

Now a different kind of tears flowed from my eyes. These were tears of relief and gratitude as I realized God had planned these details, this moment just for me. I knew he was speaking to my heart. And I realized he had been speaking all day long—through the beauty of the spring day, through the kindness of my husband, through the sweetness of strawberries for breakfast in the morning. Later God spoke even more clearly through the words of Shauna and my friend. In all of those ways he was saying, "I love you. I'm here. I want to bring you joy."

Mother's Day that year reminded me that God is always speaking. Sometimes with whispers and sometimes in more obvious ways. And even when God seems to be completely quiet, he is speaking to our hearts by listening to us. Silence is a sound all its own. Close your eyes and listen for a moment. Whatever you hear has the heartbeat of God somewhere within it. Love. Love. Love.

What My Heart Is Saying to You

Lord, I'm so glad you are always speaking in some way. Please help me hear your loving voice today in new ways. I especially need you to whisper this truth to my heart . . .

Amen.

What My Heart Is Hearing from You

Psalms 49–51

18

God Can Keep You Unharmed

Surely God is my help;
the Lord is the one who sustains me.

Psalm 54:4

She stands alone after the service ends. I've just watched her do the impossible—raise her hands in worship while her whole world is crashing down around her. I walk up next to her and gently ask, "How are you?" She answers with a voice choked by tears and the kind of smile that only comes through suffering, "It is well with my soul." I nod because I know she's telling the truth. This isn't a cliché offered like a Band-Aid to protect her heart. She means it. I put my arm around this brave woman's shoulders. As I stand there next to her, I think of the hymn that first gave us those words. They were written by a man who had just lost his four daughters in a shipwreck. He chose worship in the middle of heartbreak too.

How can we come through life's storms still saying, "It is well with my soul"? It's a mystery. And yet I've been there too. I know what it's like to stand in the eye of the hurricane and somehow know peace. Apparently David did too. He said, "[God] rescues me unharmed from the battle" (Ps. 55:18). It's not that David is in a time of serenity in his life. He's in the heat of war, the middle of a storm, surrounded by trouble. Yet he still says he's unharmed. It is well with his soul.

Dr. Henry Cloud says, "There is a big difference between *hurt* and *harm*. . . . We all hurt sometimes in facing hard truths, but it makes us grow. It can be the source of huge growth. That is not harmful. Harm is when you damage someone."[1] We will experience hurt in our lives. There's simply no way around it. And we've all seen how hurt can eventually lead to healing—like when we have surgery.

God doesn't promise we will avoid hurt. We live in a fallen, broken world, and we are not home yet.

But God will keep us from being harmed—in other words, from being irreparably damaged by what happens in our lives. That's what I saw in my friend that evening as she worshiped. I knew she'd been through many battles. Yet somehow the deepest, most eternal part of her came through unscathed. She still had hope. She still had faith. She still had an open heart. God sustained her.

It may be unwell with our bodies. It may be difficult with our families. It may be challenging with our work. Yet in all those things we can still say, "It is well with my soul." There's a place within you that this world and the enemy simply can't touch, because it's safe in the hand of God and he has promised never to let go. That's the part of you that will live forever. And while it may be dinged and dented by this life, it can't be permanently damaged.

God is faithful. He may allow hurt in our lives, but *he will not harm us*. So we can say with the apostle Paul, "I know whom I have believed, and am convinced that he is able to guard what I have entrusted to him until that day" (2 Tim. 1:12). God will sustain us until we're home with him. And on that day, we can trust it will be well with our souls . . . and with everything else too.

What My Heart Is Saying to You

Lord, you are the One who keeps my heart from being harmed. Even in the storms of life. Even when there are battles. Even on the hard days. I entrust myself to you. You also understand that this life does hurt, and I ask for your comfort today in this way . . .

Amen.

What My Heart Is Hearing from You

Psalms 52–54

19

God Notices When You Cry

Record my misery;
list my tears on your scroll—
are they not in your record?

Psalm 56:8

Letting out a sharp cry, she feels soft hands lifting her and holding her close. The first tear she sheds falls on warm skin as her mother whispers, "It's going to be okay, baby girl."

She runs across the playground and catches a stray pebble with her shoe. She tumbles down, skins her knee, and bites her bottom lip to help her be brave. But tears splash the ground beneath her anyway.

She shuts the door behind her and stands against it to take a deep breath. She looks down at the dress she's wearing—so pretty—and the words echo in her mind: "I just want to be friends." She wipes the corners of her eyes and throws the roses across the room.

She grabs hold of her husband's hand as she gives one last push. A wail fills the room and tears fill her eyes. This time they're an overflow of joy as she cradles her daughter in her arms for the first time. "Welcome, little one," she whispers. "You've got a lot of living to do."

If you could read a record of your tears, what would it contain? You probably can't even remember each one you've shed or why. But it seems God does. David trusts that all of his tears are in God's record. Why do we write things down? Because we want to remember. Because they are important to us. Because they tell a story. Perhaps all of these are reasons why God keeps our tears in his record. It's his way of telling us, "Your tears are not just water and salt to me. They are part of who you are. I value them because I love you."

Confession: I'm not much of a crier—especially in front of other people. I will fight back the tears or run away to cry alone in the bathroom. Crying feels, well, embarrassing. I don't like being vulnerable. Not to mention needy. And after all, my life is so blessed. What right do I have to boo-hoo? But clearly God doesn't feel this way about our tears. Otherwise he wouldn't record them. He'd throw them out, strike them from the book, act as if they never happened.

But instead God gives attention to our tears. In doing so, he affirms that it's okay to cry. Yes, even the mascara-smearing, snot-dripping kind of cry. I think God sees extraordinary beauty in our ugly cry. That kind of crying is what it looks like when a human heart is laid bare and open. It's what we do when we stop trying so hard to be strong. It's our way of saying, "This is too much for me." It's—dare I say it—an act of worship because we finally let ourselves be humans who need God.

So go ahead and let loose when you need to, friend. Cry when you're sad. Cry when you're happy. Cry when you're angry. And I'll try to do the same, okay? Let's dare to tell the story of our lives through our tears and remember that God, the Author of life, is treasuring each one.

What My Heart Is Saying to You

Lord, it means a lot to me that you treasure all of who I am, even my tears. Help me to express my heart to you in the sad and happy moments of my life, as well as everything in between. One thing that has made me cry lately is . . .

Amen.

What My Heart Is Hearing from You

Psalms 55–57

20

God Is Someone You Can Rely On

You are my strength, I watch for you;
you, God, are my fortress,
my God on whom I can rely.

Psalm 59:9–10

She stares at the screen and shakes her head. "I can't believe I'm watching this happen," she declares. "I rely on these people, and they're completely letting me down." She's a restaurant owner who has called in help in the form of hidden cameras to find out why her business is failing. Now thousands of other viewers are finding out right along with her as the saga unfolds on national television. One employee is stealing from her. Another snaps at customers. Others stand around playing with their cell phones instead of tending to tables. Throughout the episode the owner's emotions shift from shock to disappointment and then anger. An intervention ensues and the restaurant is restored. But it will probably be hard for her to ever trust in the same way again.

While we may not have the benefit of hidden cameras, most of us have experienced something similar. We place our trust in imperfect family members who let us down or perhaps even abuse us. We confide in friends, only to hear our secrets whispered in the halls at school the next day. We give our love to someone who says they will stay with us forever, only to wake up alone one day wondering what happened. So we decide, "I'm not relying on anyone but myself." And then comes the biggest blow: we let ourselves down too. We wonder, "Is there anyone I can truly trust?" And God whispers quietly, "Yes."

By that time it can be easy to ignore the whisper. Or even dismiss it. Just today at lunch a friend of mine discussed how often what we hope for in life doesn't turn out the way we expected. When that happens we can throw God into the same bucket as everyone else who has let us down. "See," we say, "he isn't reliable either."

But there's a big difference between God and others who have betrayed us. When we think God has disappointed us, it's usually because our circumstances haven't turned out like we planned. What we pictured in our heads and what has happened in our lives don't match. But even in those times, God himself has stayed steady in his love for us. He has not changed. He has not become undependable. He has not let us fall when he promised to catch us. People let us down because they are sinful and broken. But God is neither. That means he is fully trustworthy. "The eternal God is your refuge, and underneath are the everlasting arms" (Deut. 33:27).

Not only is he reliable, but he understands that nothing else in our lives is the same way. He understands that we'll be disappointed and betrayed. He knows that our expectations will not be met. That gives him great compassion for us. And it's in the very moment we may want to push him away that he wants to say, "Come here. Lean on me. Put the full weight of your need on me. I can handle it. I love you, and I will not let you down." God sits behind the hidden camera that shows every angle of our lives. "So we know and rely on the love God has for us" (1 John 4:16). He knows the reality, and he's the only One who can make it right in our hearts again. And he will.

What My Heart Is Saying to You

Lord, you know the disappointments I've experienced. That sometimes makes it hard to trust. But I believe you when you say you're there for me. Today I'm leaning on you for . . .

Amen.

What My Heart Is Hearing from You

Psalms 58–60

21

God Is Your Protector

Because you are my help,
I sing in the shadow of your wings.

Psalm 63:7

The high-pitched chirp startles me. It's quickly followed by the familiar "woof!" of my beagle-basset hound in the backyard. I jump up from my chair and race to the door. It's spring, and operation "rescue baby birdies" has officially started. I find a small sparrow cornered by my dog. My canine has a look of pride on her face, as if to say, "I just saved your life. You can thank me later."

I beckon my four-legged friend away from the bird and find something to gently lift it with that won't leave my scent behind. Before our neighbors had pets, we used to lob the little chirpers over the fence, where they'd gently land like fluffy softballs. But now all the bordering yards pose threats too. So the sparrow gets a trip to the front yard where she can hide out in our thick bushes. Her mama follows close behind, and I make sure the two have found each other again before I go back inside. I can just imagine what that mother bird is thinking: "I wish you, fuzzy bird baby, were still small enough to fit safely in the nest under my wing."

While we often think of God as our heavenly Father, he describes himself in mothering terms at times—especially as a bird who gathers her chicks under her wings. That metaphor is used repeatedly in Psalms, and Jesus later laments that he would like to gather Jerusalem under his wings but they are not willing. I love this picture of God's care for us, because at the heart of it is this: the bird with her little ones under her wings is essentially putting herself between her young and any predators. She's saying, "You want to come after my children? You're going to have to come through me first." It's not a distant defensive strategy. It's up-close, personal, and powerful. It means that she's willing to die to make sure those she cares for are ultimately okay.

And that's exactly what Jesus did for us. He put himself between us and our sin, between us and the enemy, between us and this world. He stretched out on a cross, and with his arms spread wide like wings, he said that we could all come there for protection. It seems this is especially true in hard times. The verse above doesn't say, "in the light of your wings." It says "in the shadow." When darkness comes to our lives, what we tend to notice is the absence of light. But what if we see it differently? What if we see that the darkness isn't darkness at all. Instead it's the shadow of God's wing over us. When it's hard to see, it may be because he's placing himself between us and some threat. To lift the darkness at that moment would be to expose us to something far more dreadful.

I don't understand pain. I don't know all the reasons it happens. I don't know how your situation will be resolved. I don't know how mine will either. But I'd like to think that sometimes the silent, stifling places we beg God to get us out of can actually be his covering over us from something far worse. Yes, life is difficult and hard things happen. Yet how much more so would it be if we didn't have God's protection?

We will never know all God has shielded us from, at least not this side of heaven. What we do know and can trust in with all our hearts is that he was willing to die on a cross to protect us. And that means he's committed to our well-being. Will we understand? Probably not. Does that take the hurt away? Not this side of heaven. But it does mean that instead of striving so hard, we can quiet our hearts, nestle in to the side of the One who loves us, and listen to his heartbeat while we wait for what seeks to destroy us to pass. Maybe sometimes we can even dare to sing

What My Heart Is Saying to You

Lord, thank you for hiding me in the shadow of your wings. It's amazing to know you've said you'll put yourself between me and whatever threatens to harm me. Even if it costs your life. Today I need you to protect my heart in this way . . .

Amen.

What My Heart Is Hearing from You

Psalms 61–63

22

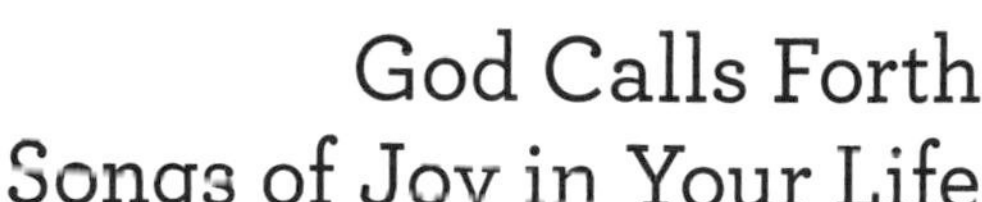

God Calls Forth Songs of Joy in Your Life

The whole earth is filled with awe at
your wonders;
where morning dawns,
where evening fades,
you call forth songs of joy.

Psalm 65:8

She watched her parents do drugs in the kitchen. She once ate a stick of lip balm to hold off hunger pains. She learned how to live on the streets. And then she went to Harvard. Liz Murray's story doesn't have the ending you would expect. Her memoir, *Breaking*

Night, is aptly titled because that's what she did. She didn't give in or give up. Instead she made it through the dark of her life and saw dawn come. She broke the night in her life rather than letting it break her.

Stories like Liz's captivate us because we want to break the night too. At first the darkness comes softly. Perhaps we get bad news from the doctor. Our marriage begins to feel a little off. Or our employer announces that there will be changes. But then the twilight deepens until we can hardly see. What happened to the light in our lives? Then it's midnight and morning seems so far away. It's in those moments that we're most tempted to give in to the sleep of the heart—the place where we're alive but not really living. It would be so much easier not to feel, not to keep believing, just to shut our eyes and forget it all.

But instead we grit our teeth and cry out to God and hold on with all our might. We keep loving. We keep persevering. We keep choosing what's hard even though it would be so much easier just to give in.

Then the moment comes, the first sliver of light just over the horizon. Our eyes can hardly take it in because they've been used to the dark so long. But slowly it appears. At first it's just fingers of light stretching toward us. Then the sun barely slips over the horizon.

We catch our breath because we'd forgotten the world could actually be beautiful. Then it hits us: we've made it through the worst. We've broken night.

It's in that place—"where morning dawns, where evening fades"—that God calls forth "songs of joy." Whose songs are they?

Those songs are ours because we've survived. They're the sound of our soul declaring God is good no matter what.

They're the songs of the angels, perhaps, as they see our victory.

They're the songs of the encouragers who have walked with us in the night.

And I believe they're even the songs of God himself. "The Lord your God is with you, the Mighty Warrior who saves. He will take great delight in you; in his love he will no longer rebuke you, but will rejoice over you with singing" (Zeph. 3:17).

You may walk through nights so dark that they seem as if they will never end. Your heart may seem as silent as a stone. You may forget what it even means to feel joy for a season. But dawn will come. And you will sing again. That's the hope. That's the promise. That's the reason to keep your heart awake just a little bit longer.

What My Heart Is Saying to You

Lord, it would be so easy to let my heart drift off to sleep so I could stop feeling this hurt. Please help me stay awake—to you, to life, to love. I believe that the dawn is coming and I will sing again. And even in the dark I choose to praise you for . . .

Amen.

What My Heart Is Hearing from You

Psalms 64–66

23

God Will Bear Your Burdens

Praise be to the Lord, to God our Savior,
who daily bears our burdens.

Psalm 68:19

When my husband and I go trekking through airports, he inevitably ends up with my giant tote bag on top of his rolling suitcase. It's so common he now reaches for it as soon as we get out of our car. I smile and hand it over so we can continue on our way. I can handle my suitcase, but the added weight of another bag tends to slow me down. When we were first married, I resisted the extra help. I wanted to be the perfect wife (aka no needs), and so I'd heft my bag onto my arm and stroll into the airport. "Do you want me to get that?" my husband would ask. "No, no, I'm fine. I've just dislocated my shoulder. No big deal." Over time I learned this: letting someone meet your needs is part of letting them love you.

We all have times in our lives when what we need to carry through life is just too much for us to handle on our own. We're good at looking strong and trying to hide the fact that we're about to fall over. We wave away offers of assistance and plaster on a fake smile instead. But we're not intended to go through life that way. We need others to bear our burdens, especially when we're hurting. And amazingly, God himself says in the verse above that he will daily help us with them.

Of course, there are other times when my requests for help aren't coming from an actual need. Instead I just want what I want. That's when I start whining. Something that I should legitimately be carrying by myself gets tossed to someone else just because I don't feel like dealing with it anymore. When I try to hand over my microscopic purse to my husband to carry in public, he just raises his eyebrows and politely shakes his head. No ma'am. He wisely knows when I truly can't handle something and when I'm just being silly.

Scripture gives us a distinction between those two as well. In *Strong Women, Soft Hearts* author Paula Rinehart explains:

> In one verse, Paul instructs us to bear each other's *burdens*, which means those heavy boulders of responsibility or pain that befall every person from time to time. We are to share the extra heavy trials of life. Right in the same chapter, however, Paul makes a curious statement: "Each man must bear his own *load*." That sounds contradictory until you realize that the word for load means "knapsack." Each of us has a knapsack to carry through life that is uniquely our own.[1]

In other words, we've got to pull our weight in life, but there's a limit. We're not expected to take on more than we can handle alone. God is committed to carrying our burdens—what we can't carry by ourselves. Often he does this through other people. But we have to be willing to ask for and receive the help, which can be scary.

Somehow it's easy to confuse *having* a burden with *being* a burden. That leads to fear that we'll be too much for people. But the two are not the same. Your burdens are not your identity. They're temporary baggage. And when you let someone come alongside you and use their strength on your behalf, you're letting them love you. You're affirming their value in your life. You're saying that you trust them with something important to you.

It's okay to say, "I can't hold this up anymore. Can you please help me?" To do so is part of receiving *and* giving love. Whatever you're going through, you don't have to bear the full weight of it. God is ready and willing to bear your burdens so you can continue your journey. And he'll send others to help you too.

What My Heart Is Saying to You

Lord, it's easy to pretend that I don't need help. And admitting I do can be downright scary. But it's true. So I'm coming to you today with this burden I need you to bear for me. It is . . .

Amen.

What My Heart Is Hearing from You

Psalms 67–69

24

God Will Deliver You

From birth I have relied on you;
you brought me forth from my
mother's womb.
I will ever praise you. . . .
My lips will shout for joy
when I sing praise to you—
I whom you have delivered.

Psalm 71:6, 23

The text pops onto my phone saying, "We're heading to the hospital. Please pray for a painless and easy delivery!" Hours later another text appears. It includes a name, weight, and picture of a brand-new baby girl. She's absolutely beautiful. Her little face still bears the marks of labor. Painless and easy? Not for baby or mama. But worth it? Absolutely.

Our first delivery happens when we're born. You probably don't even know the name of the doctor who delivered you. But it doesn't matter, because it turns out he or she was just a secondary player in the scene. David tells us in the psalm above that God himself brought you forth from your mother's womb. He caught you with unseen hands and welcomed you to the world. And he's been delivering you ever since.

"God, please give me a painless and easy delivery!" we pray when trouble comes. But that's not the way delivery works. There's always pressure in the process. Quite a bit of darkness. And it seems to take much longer than we anticipated. Yet just when it seems we can't take any more, it's over. Only from that place can we say, "It was all worth it."

My friend recently had a baby, and she told me about one of the sessions in the birthing class she and her husband did together. She said that every woman who has a child will have a moment when the delivery seems like too much for her. No matter how much she has planned and prepared, it will catch her by surprise. In that moment, every reasonable thought will flee from her mind and be taken over by a single one: make the pain stop. That time is the hardest for the baby too. The teacher of the birthing class said the only way to get through that is to know it's going to happen. Because then you realize it won't last forever. And once it's over, you're through the worst of it.

We need to know that when our hearts are in delivery too. There will come a time when every truth you've ever heard will seem to ring hollow. You will forget everything you've ever heard about how God is good. You will not believe that you're going to make it. This one thought will come again and again: make the pain stop. By knowing that time will come, we can push through to the other side. We can somehow cling to the promise that God is there and he will deliver us. And that pain really can lead to new life.

God is your deliverer.

He brought you forth from your mother's womb when you took your first breath.

He delivers you in the hard moments when it feels as if you will never catch your breath again.

And he will deliver you from this life to the next when you take your final breath and enter eternity with him.

What My Heart Is Saying to You

Lord, thank you for being my deliverer. From my first breath to my last, you are the One I can trust to always see me through. I commit myself into your hands. Please deliver me from . . .

Amen.

What My Heart Is Hearing from You

Psalms 70–72

25

God Is Your Piece of the Pie

My flesh and my heart may fail,
but God is the strength of my heart
and my portion forever.

Psalm 73:26

The pie sits in all its glory behind the glass case. Over lunch my friend and I stare at it with anticipation. Peanut butter. Whipped cream. Golden crust. Soon it will be ours. It's a tradition for us to share a slice when we come to this restaurant. And then at the last minute, we watch as a server reaches in and takes the last piece. "Noooooo," we wail. "That's *our* piece." This may seem a bit dramatic, but then again, you've never tasted that pie, have you? You'd wail too. I'm just saying.

My friend and I look forlornly at our plates and then begin to giggle at ourselves. We laugh because it's a moment when we remember what it means to be human—to long for something (sometimes quite silly) and then to be devastated when we don't get it.

Asaph, the writer of the psalm above, describes how he went through a period of deep frustration in his life. This was about far more than pie. Everywhere he looked it seemed like the wicked were getting the good stuff while he was left empty-handed. "What gives?" he seemed to ask God. "I follow you faithfully, yet those who act like you don't even exist are getting my slice." Then Asaph makes a trip to the temple and his perspective changes. He realizes what the ungodly are getting is ultimately temporary and unsatisfying. He finally declares, "God is the strength of my heart and my portion forever."

When we're going through a hard time, it's easy to be like Asaph. We start looking at those around us and believing everyone else has it better than we do.

Her piece of pie is a perfect body.

Her piece of pie is an insanely happy marriage.

Her piece of pie is a house that could be in a Pottery Barn catalog.

Of course, all of these are exaggerations, and we don't know the full story that might be unfolding in what looks like an ideal life. But pain can skew our perspective. Then we begin to feel like God is holding out on us. We've been so faithful, and then he just gives the piece of pie we deserve to someone else (insert whining here if you're like me).

Yet God walks around the corner with a plate in his hand and says, "I saved this for you. It's the best piece of all. It's your portion." And what he offers is astounding. The God of the universe gives us himself. He is *I Am*. That means in whatever circumstance, he is what we need.

I Am peace when the doctor delivers bad news.

I Am hope when one more month goes by and you're not pregnant.

I Am strength when it feels like you can't go on another day.

God is our portion, and here's the best part: he can never be consumed. There will always be more of him for whatever we need. Our hearts never have to go hungry, because we can always say the prayer he loves to answer: "More of you, please."

What My Heart Is Saying to You

Lord, I'm so grateful you are my portion forever. I pray that you will help me to see all the ways you fill my heart with what I need. Please give me more of you in this area of my life today . . .

Amen.

What My Heart Is Hearing from You

Psalms 73–75

26

God Is Preparing You

He chose David his servant
and took him from the sheep pens;
from tending the sheep he brought him
to be the shepherd of his people
Jacob,
of Israel his inheritance.
And David shepherded them with
integrity of heart;
with skillful hands he led them.

Psalm 78:70–72

When you look at my friend Cari Kaufman, you instantly notice her warm eyes and bright smile. She's a natural encourager with a laugh that makes you want to join in whatever conversation she's having. She loves to be on stage speaking or acting in ways that make a difference. But years ago she found herself at the center of a completely different scene.

One evening Cari saw a group of young men attacking a girl. Most of us would have run or simply called 911, but Cari took action and dispatched several of the aggressors on her own. She received the prestigious Soldier's Medal for Heroism as a result of her bravery. While Cari says she responded even without having time to think through each action, she had unknowingly been preparing for that moment for years. Because of her physical and military training, she knew what to do, and she did it with extraordinary courage.

I imagine the training Cari went through wasn't always fun. Surely there were times when her body ached, her muscles were sore, and watching television sounded like a much better idea. When we're going through challenges, often what we see most is the here and now. Why is God stretching us so much? What's the point of this weight we're bearing? How come other people seem to have it easier? Yet usually what God is doing in our lives is not just about this moment—and it's certainly not just about us.

Perhaps David had similar thoughts as he did the dirty and demanding work of taking care of sheep in the desert. His brothers were off at battle while he got left behind. Yet in the quietness of those vast pastures, God was training David for his moment. David learned to fight lions. He knew how to battle a bear. He had already decided to lay down his life for his sheep if necessary. So when a giant named Goliath challenged the army of Israel, David was the only one willing to step forward with a sling and a stone. He didn't know this moment was coming, but he had been preparing for it for years.

David would fight many more battles in the decades to come. He would also become king—the anointed shepherd of God's people. So much of what he did as a wise ruler and brave warrior actually began back in a lonely place with a few sheep and many frustrations.

So if you find yourself in a season of life where you can't understand what God is doing, it may be that he's training and preparing you. Stay with it, friend. Finish what he's asked you to do or go through. Persevere. God has more ahead for you than you can even imagine. And when your moment to save a life (or a soul), slay a giant, or be used by God in some other unexpected way comes, you'll be ready.

What My Heart Is Saying to You

Lord, thank you that you see the future and know everything that's going to come into my life. I'm glad you can prepare me for what's ahead even when the challenges I'm facing now don't make sense. Please give me the strength to persevere in . . .

Amen.

What My Heart Is Hearing from You

Psalms 76–78

27

God Doesn't Need Conditions in Your Life to Be Right

But you would be fed with the finest of
wheat;
with honey from the rock I would
satisfy you.

Psalm 81:16

I grew up an hour from NASA headquarters in Texas. As the time for a space shuttle launch came closer, the local news would buzz with all the latest updates. My family and I would wait in anticipation to see when the latest venture into space would begin. We loved hearing the countdown and then the declaration of "Liftoff!" as the rockets roared to life and the shuttle disappeared from sight in the blue skies above.

Many of those launches were preceded by delays. NASA would send out a report that "conditions weren't right" and announce a new launch date. It always amazed me that some of the most brilliant scientists in the world still had to stand by for simple factors like weather and wind.

We can tend to think of God the same way. We imagine "conditions have to be right" for him to work in our lives. So when he doesn't launch the plan we'd hoped for on our schedule, we can begin to take matters into our own hands to fix it. We think, "If only I can get my act together, then surely God will do this for me." Or, "If I can just try a whole lot harder, then he'll notice." Maybe even, "If I'm perfect, then nothing can stop God's plan for my life." But we soon realize our efforts are about as effective as trying to control the weather.

And even more than that, they're unnecessary because God isn't limited by circumstances. In the psalm above, he says that if his people are faithful to him, he will satisfy them with "honey from the rock." Honey? From a rock? What about the flowers and the bees and the hive? It seems all of the conditions honey would normally require are irrelevant to God. If he wants his people to have honey, then any old rock will do. God does what he wants when he wants.

That leads to the question: then why hasn't he launched my rocket already? What's he waiting for? And here's my very spiritual answer: I have no earthly idea. But it's not because you've somehow goofed up the conditions of your life so much that he can't possibly work. It's not because he's busy doing something else. Most of all, it's not because he doesn't care.

God's ways are not like ours. He has unlimited perspective on all of eternity, and that's so much more than we can see. Even NASA's best are still limited in their ability to know what's happening in the universe. They have to guess sometimes. But never God. So if he's delaying your launch, you can trust there's a reason. And whatever else it might involve, that reason always includes love.

You can have hope, because when God's perfect timing does come, absolutely nothing can stand in his way. Not the weather. Not your imperfections. Not this fallen, broken world. Nothing.

One day you'll hear in your heart the countdown begin and the exclamation of "Liftoff!" from deep within. Then you'll soar in ways you never knew you could. And the conditions won't just be right—they'll be extraordinary.

What My Heart Is Saying to You

Lord, sometimes your timing in my life is hard to understand. I'm so glad I can trust that you don't need the "right conditions" for your plan to work. You have no limits. Please do this "impossible" thing in my life . . .

Amen.

What My Heart Is Hearing from You

Psalms 79–81

28

God Has a Great Place for You Today

Better is one day in your courts
than a thousand elsewhere;
I would rather be a doorkeeper in the house of my God
than dwell in the tents of the wicked.

Psalm 84:10

In our area we have a yearly "parade of homes." In other words, for one weekend we get to invade the houses of strangers and openly stare at their kitchens, living rooms, and closets. The idea is that architects, interior designers, and proud homeowners get to show off their hard work and the public gets to be inspired. I remember tromping through a mansion one year. The value was well over a million dollars. Dark wood cabinets combined with granite countertops and beautiful overhead beams took my breath away.

I thought for a moment, "What would it be like to live in a place like this?" Imagine if in that moment someone had come up to me and said, "I'll give you this house right now. There's only one condition: your family can't live with you." In a second all the appeal of that home would have vanished and I would have replied, "A house is nothing without the people I love."

I imagine you would have answered in the same way. (Okay, okay—we all have days when living by ourselves seems a bit appealing, or at least more peaceful, but most of the time it would be an easy decision.) We know somewhere deep inside that a house may have walls, but to become a home it needs love.

Yet we can look around us and begin to go on a "parade of lives." We peer into one woman's existence and wish we had her social life. Or we spend time with another and walk away longing for a career like hers. Maybe we admire a friend's role at church and wish we could trade. But doing so would be like accepting the mansion with the condition we talked about in the beginning. And here's why: *God is where you are right now.* If you were to walk away from his will for you, it might seem as if you were living in a better "house," but he would not be there. So it would never be a place where your heart could be at home and find rest.

I returned from the parade of homes that day with a new perspective. I saw the scratched-up kitchen table where friends laughed with us. I saw the unmade bed where my husband wakes up next to me in the morning. I saw the needs-to-be-swept back porch where I watch the sun slip behind the trees and the fireflies come out. Other places in my house held painful memories. Yet all of them were newly beautiful to me—not because they were the biggest and best, but because they represented the life God had for me.

"Better is one day in your courts than a thousand elsewhere" (Ps. 84:10). In other words, better is one day in the center of God's will than a thousand in a mansion of your own making. Wherever you are in this moment, God is with you. And even in the hard places, you are living under the extravagant shelter of his love.

What My Heart Is Saying to You

Lord, it brings my heart great comfort to know that wherever I am today, you are there too. Better is one day where you want me than a thousand in the "best" place I could dream up. I ask for your help being content with . . .

Amen.

What My Heart Is Hearing from You

Psalms 82–84

29

God Has Compassion on You

But you, Lord, are a compassionate and
gracious God,
slow to anger, abounding in love and
faithfulness.

Psalm 86:15

The phone rings and I don't recognize the number. I pick it up, and after a quick hello a nurse begins giving me test results. I can hardly understand a lot of the medical words she's using, but I do catch "autoimmune disease" and "referral to a specialist."

I thank her for the call and hang up with my head spinning. The months of fatigue and feeling unwell might have a reason behind them after all.

When I began growing tired more easily than I used to, my response was usually to tell myself, "You're fine! Keep going! Other people have a lot more on their plate than you do and they're handling it." As you can imagine, those little pep talks did little to restore my energy, and I finally felt weary enough to go to a doctor.

When the nurse told me the results of that visit, it was interesting how my dialogue with myself quickly changed. I began to say, "You need to take care of yourself. You've been doing so much for so long. Why don't you rest for a bit?" That phone call from the doctor didn't give me answers, but it did give me something I lacked: self-compassion.

As I walked through the doors of the specialist's office the next day, I could sense the prayers of friends with me. When I had blood drawn, I turned my head and closed my eyes. I talked to Jesus. And it seemed he whispered in response, "I love you. I'm with you. No matter what, you will be okay."

I realized that he had been talking to me like this all along.

While I told myself, "Get over it," he had been whispering, "Come to me, all you who are weary and burdened, and I will give you rest" (Matt. 11:28). While I asked myself, "What's the matter with you?" he continued to remind me that whatever was troubling me mattered to him. While I challenged myself to simply try harder, he invited me to try grace instead.

We are often far less compassionate to ourselves than God is to us.

What are you saying to yourself right now about the hard time you're experiencing? Would you say those words to a close friend you love? Then don't say them to your heart either. God is on your side, and that means you can be too.

I still don't know what's going on with my body. It's frustrating to know I need to go more slowly. I want to race, not rest. And yet in the quietness that's coming into my life, I'm finally hearing words from the heart of God I desperately need. Ever so slowly, they're replacing what I've been saying to myself for so long. So I'm praying I learn to embrace more grace, to lean into love, to rest in the arms of the One who has great compassion for me. And for you too.

What My Heart Is Saying to You

Lord, you are so gracious and compassionate. Thank you for never being harsh with my heart but instead extending kindness to me in every circumstance. Help me do the same with myself more often. I need to remember that . . .

Amen.

What My Heart Is Hearing from You

Psalms 85–87

30

God Knows Your Calendar

Teach us to number our days,
that we may gain a heart of wisdom.
Psalm 90:12

The same calendar has been hanging on my grandfather's wall for over a decade. A single day in December is circled. It's the day my grandmother, his wife of more than fifty years, went home to heaven. I have a similar calendar hanging in my heart. There's a day circled in April when our baby slipped to the arms of Jesus after a few weeks of life. And I've known others who have circled the days of a diagnosis or divorce. As humans, we seem to have a longing to mark the days that mark us.

When we think of those days, it changes the way we look at all the ones that are yet to come. They remind us that life is finite and fragile. In the busy, happy seasons we can forget that's true. We fight with the people we love like we'll have forever to make it right. We squander hours on meaningless activities as if we have more than enough time to fulfill our purpose. We drift through life on autopilot and forget that every mile is bringing us closer to the end of our journey.

Then a day ends up circled on the calendar, and suddenly we're jolted awake. We see the blue sky. We hug the people who are close to us. We treat time like treasure instead of trash. That's the hidden gift of trouble: it makes all that's good and beautiful and true stand out like stars in a night sky. We learn to count our blessings and to make our days count. Over time we become wise because we realize that everything we value is just a breath from being gone.

The people I know who have grasped this truth the most don't live in fear. Instead they're made courageous in a wild and rare way. They embrace life with both hands and yet at the same time hold it loosely. They overflow with joy and weep with abandon. They love deeply and yet know how to let people go. They see those circles on the calendar as part of a much bigger circle—one that goes on for all eternity.

Our lives are a paradox: so short and yet eternal. We have so little time and yet we have forever. We are temporary and yet we are going to be around a million years from now. Wisdom is what lets us live between those paradoxes. It sets all that happens in the calendar of eternity. It gives us the grace to appreciate the "now" while anticipating the "then." And to live somewhere in between.

Live like this day will never come again. Because it won't.

And live like you will exist forever. Because you will.

We're all somewhere between now and not yet, sustained by the only One who holds the hands of time . . . and our hearts too.

What My Heart Is Saying to You

Lord, teach me to number my days that I may gain a heart of wisdom. I pray you will help me embrace the present while also looking forward to forever with you. Today I'm wondering . . .

Amen.

What My Heart Is Hearing from You

Psalms 88–90

31

God Will Help You Trample Trouble

You will tread on the lion and the cobra;
you will trample the great lion and
the serpent.

Psalm 91:13

When my parents recently bought land in the wide-open expanse of Texas, my mom had a request. She wanted to go shoe shopping. That might not sound like it's out of the ordinary for any woman. But my petite mama had a special kind of footwear in mind: snake boots. No, not the kind made from a snake. I mean boots made in a such way that a feisty rattlesnake can't get his fangs into them. Yes, ma'am. Don't mess with Texas—or with Texas mamas.

While it might spook you to think about walking in a place with a snake, you actually do it every day. All the way back in Eden, a serpent appeared with one purpose in mind: to deceive Eve. His cunning worked, and mankind chose sin. But when Jesus died on the cross, he crushed the enemy. What began in Eden ended at Calvary. And because of Jesus, we can stomp on evil when it comes our way too. We've all got a pair of snake boots for our souls.

Sometimes we forget that we have the power to trample trouble. We catch a glimpse of the enemy and we run for our lives. But we have been given what we need to stand firm. James 4:7 says, "Submit yourselves, then, to God. Resist the devil, and he will flee from you." That's a two-step process. First align yourself with God (that's like putting on your snake boots), and then resist the devil.

How do we resist that tricky serpent? The same way Jesus did—with God's Word. Eve fell prey to one question: "Did God really say . . .?" And when the enemy tried to tempt Jesus, he used "if" statements.

Same tactic, different words. In both cases, he was trying to introduce just enough doubt to expose a vulnerable part of the heart. Then he'd have the opportunity to strike. He still does the same with us. So we learn a lesson from Eve and instead answer with God's Word like Jesus did. We reply, "Yes, God really did say . . . ," because nothing can defeat God's declarations. We "tread on the cobra and trample the serpent" with truth.

I hope my mama never encounters a rattlesnake. But if she does, I have a feeling she'll be prepared. After all, she did have to wake me up to go to school for several years. And that's pretty close. I imagine back in those days she would have loved some teenager-proof boots. Can I get an "amen"?

No matter what you encounter today from the enemy, you've got what you need not only to step over trouble but to stomp it to bits.

So don't let your fear get in the way.

Instead, as Texans like to say, "Go get 'em, girl."

What My Heart Is Saying to You

Lord, thank you for defeating the enemy forever on the cross. Help me to courageously live in victory today. I pray you will help me stomp on the lie that . . .

Amen.

What My Heart Is Hearing from You

Psalms 91–93

32

God Will Ease Your Anxiety

When anxiety was great within me,
your consolation brought me joy.

Psalm 94:19

She takes a deep breath and pulls on her swim cap. The pool stretches out before her. The lane seems longer than it did in practice. Her little hands tremble at her sides and her eyes grow wide. In a moment, she'll take her place on the starting block.

With little time to spare, her coach rushes to her side. He leans down and looks into her eyes. "You can do this. You're going to be okay. You know how to finish this race." She nods and enthusiasm replaces the insecurity. When the race begins, she leaps into the water without hesitation and swims steadily all the way. Her face is full of joy as she pops up from the water at the other end.

How can we go from anxiety to excitement or joy so quickly, especially as children? It turns out those two emotions are closely related in our brains. Both are states of heightened arousal. Think about a time when you were nervous and one when you were elated. Both times you were probably more aware of everything around you—the sights, sounds, and smells. You probably also remember the details of those events more clearly than others. In times of both anxiety and joy, our bodies produce adrenaline. We feel more energized so that we can engage in whatever is about to happen. We're on "high alert" and fully tuned in to what's happening, both internally and externally.

So I love that this Psalm above doesn't just say, "When anxiety was great within me, you calmed me down." Nope. God doesn't take us from anxiety to calm. He can actually take us from anxiety to joy. How does he do that? Truth can switch the track in our minds. When we remember what God says, we change courses from thoughts that lead to anxiety to those that can instead lead to emotions like courage and even celebration. For example, you might feel fear about an upcoming meeting at work. And yet as you pray and remember what God has told you is true, you find yourself becoming first calmer and then even filled with confidence and anticipation.

We're human, and for our brains to learn to respond in new ways takes time and practice. But we can begin to change by saying, "Okay, I'm feeling anxious. That's okay. It's the same system that's related to a lot of other things—like enthusiasm and joy. God, please help me pinpoint the thoughts that are causing fear and replace them with faith instead so my emotions can change too." This won't happen instantly, and that's totally fine. God understands. Yet as you practice this transformation, over time you will probably notice a little less anxiety and a little more excitement coming into your life.

Instead of immediately running away, see some of the moments when you feel anxiety as opportunities to retrain your brain. Lean into them. Learn from them. And let them eventually lead you to more joy.

What My Heart Is Saying to You

Lord, you are the only One who can turn my anxiety into joy. You understand how my brain works. Thank you that I'm fearfully and wonderfully made. Help me to respond in new ways, especially in this situation . . .

Amen.

What My Heart Is Hearing from You

Psalms 94–96

33

God Is Bigger Than Your Problems

The mountains melt like wax before
the Lord,
before the Lord of all the earth.

Psalm 97:5

It's a clear summer morning and my husband and I are joining our friends for a bike ride. But before you picture cushy seats and little baskets on the front of our bikes, let me give you a little background. My husband does one-hundred-mile bike races. Yes, one hundred. And I've learned this means his idea of "far" and "steep climb" are a little different than mine. He and my friend's husband decide that today they will take their wives to what's known as Tower Hill. It's a stretch of road that winds upward for a significant distance. Reaching the top is a bit of a badge of honor in our area. And for whatever reason, they believe we're ready.

The first few miles of our ride go by pleasantly, and then we find ourselves at the base of Tower Hill. I stare up at it, try to maintain momentum, and then begin to pedal. I hear the theme song to the movie *Rocky* in my mind. I grind through every gear I have. I use every bit of muscle I've got. By now I've lost sight of my husband. I arrogantly assume he's somewhere behind me. When I finally reach the top (yes, I made it to the top!) I discover him leaning on his bike and sipping water with a smile on his face as if we'd just completed a walk in the park. Seriously?

To Mark, Tower Hill is "no big deal." It's just another hill. But to me it felt like Mount Everest. The difference was our experience and perspective. The same is true when it comes to how God sees the mountains we have to overcome in our lives. We look at them and think, "How am I ever going to get past this thing?" while God looks at them and they "melt like wax" before him. God is not surprised, intimidated, or discouraged by your mountains. He has the perspective of all of history as well as eternity. And as intense as what you're facing may feel, he's dealt with far worse and beat it.

Does this mean God tells us, "Just get over it"? No, that's the beautiful part. He comes alongside us and encourages our hearts every bit of the climb. He doesn't wait at the top, sipping water and saying, "Well, that was easy," while we struggle. What changed climbing Tower Hill for me in the future was having my husband by my side. I told him, "Look, I know you can race up this hill in nothing flat. But I need you beside me. You might even toss me an encouraging word or two along the way." He grinned, and next time we went, sure enough, he stayed by my side. The climb remained just as intense and yet somehow felt less grueling. I knew I would make it and that I would not be alone.

What mountain are you facing today? Whatever it is, God is bigger. He's strong enough to overcome it. And gentle enough to ride beside you. When I ride up Tower Hill now, I still start wishing my husband had the power to flatten mountains at a certain point. But I also realize I won't become stronger by sticking to flat ground. It's the struggle that reshapes us.

Yes, God could level that mountain in your life in a minute. Why he doesn't will probably remain a mystery until heaven. But you can know this: your mountain is revealing courage you never knew you had and creating more power within you. The next mountain you face isn't going to feel as steep as this one. Not because it will be smaller but because you will be stronger. And God will be with you all the way to the top.

What My Heart Is Saying to You

Lord, even the tallest mountain in my life is small to you. Please give me the strength to make it over this steep place. Stay by me, and if you should so choose, turn this mountain into flat ground. But no matter what, I will keep going because . . .

Amen.

What My Heart Is Hearing from You

Psalms 97–99

34

God Calls You His Own

Know that the Lord is God.
It is he who made us, and we are his;
we are his people, the sheep of his pasture.

Psalm 100:3

She hands me a bundle wrapped in blue. As I peer inside I see eyes the same shade as mom's and hair with a bit of wave like dad's. I smile and say, "Well, there's no doubt he's yours." She grins and begins to tell me about other family characteristics already showing up in his sweet face.

I've had many conversations like the one above with new parents. It seems one of the first questions to come up is always, "Who does he look like?" There's something beautifully satisfying about seeing in our children what we know in our hearts: they belong to us.

We're made in the image of God, and I wonder if he sometimes has the same kind of conversations with the angels about us. "See that one? She's got my eyes. And her over there? Her heartbeat is so much like mine."

I've heard preachers pound the pulpit and declare, "You are not your own!" They're trying to warn us away from living selfish lives. They seem to imply God "owns" us the way people own any ordinary object. But I don't think that's what God means when he tells us we are his. I believe God's affirmation of his ownership of us is much more like a parent with a child. He's saying, "You belong to me."

That distinction matters, because if we simply "own" something, then it's ours to use. When something "belongs" to us, then we're responsible for its care. In the psalm above, the writer says we're not only God's people but also "the sheep of his pasture." In ancient times, the members of a shepherd's flock were a lot like his children. Without his loving attention, protection, and provision, the sheep would get lost, become malnourished, or even die. A good shepherd, like a parent, loved his sheep so much that he would even be willing to lay down his life for them.

In hard times, we can take comfort in knowing we are watched over by someone who loves us. We're not drifting through life on our own. We're not orphans or sheep without a shepherd. We have a home. We have an identity. We have someone who is committed to our care. That means we don't have to try so hard to fend for ourselves. We don't have to go through life believing no one will be there for us. We don't have to carry the weight of our own existence.

Instead we can come to our heavenly Father, our Good Shepherd, and say, "I belong to you. You've promised to take care of me. Will you please help me?" He will always answer that prayer. And you have many other brothers and sisters, fellow sheep in the flock, who can come alongside you too.

You're not on your own.

And you're not simply "owned."

You're deeply loved and cherished as part of a family and flock forever.

What My Heart Is Saying to You

Lord, I'm so glad I belong to you. I'm grateful for your care, and it brings me so much comfort to know that I will never be on my own. Will you please help me with the following situation today?

Amen.

What My Heart Is Hearing from You

Psalms 100–102

35

God Has Benefits Planned for You

Praise the Lord*, my soul,*
and forget not all his benefits—
who forgives all your sins
and heals all your diseases,
who redeems your life from the pit
and crowns you with love and
compassion,
who satisfies your desires with good things

Psalm 103:2–5

She's considering several different job options. They come with similar salaries and day-to-day duties. She says, "I'm taking a hard look at what I really value. Do I want overtime pay or extra vacation? It would be nice to work somewhere with endless benefits!" I nod my head and laugh with her as we begin listing off what we'd choose: free cupcakes, endless coffee, a personal trainer (to make up for the cupcakes). I actually did briefly work at a software company that offered everything from free gourmet coffee to massages. But here's the thing: no matter where we are, the work piles up after a while, and we can tend to forget about the benefits.

Perhaps that kind of forgetfulness inspired King David to write this psalm. He had served God and Israel for years by the time he penned these words. He'd seen his share of war, betrayal, and family trouble. What had started as a glorious appointing probably felt routine on many days—especially the hard ones.

We can tend to feel the same about whatever is in our lives, work or otherwise. When we first get married, have a baby, or join a new church, it's easy to see the benefits. Then tough times come and we lose our perspective. It can be time to say with David, "Praise the Lord, my soul, and forget not all his benefits."

After that introduction, David goes on to list the specific benefits that mean the most to him:

God forgives sins. Perhaps David thought of his affair with Bathsheba on this one.

God heals all your diseases. Maybe a time of serious illness came to mind.

God redeems your life from the pit. David could have remembered how he came from a low position to become king.

God crowns you with love and compassion. After many years, battles, and mistakes, David valued these characteristics of God more than any of the royal perks.

Let's talk through your own list of benefits for a bit too.

Think back to when you became a believer. What changed about your life?

Reflect on your present situation. How has God helped and sustained you?

Consider the future. How will he be there for you no matter what happens?

We're human and we naturally grow used to what's in our lives. It can all seem ordinary until we intentionally refocus on the extraordinary benefits God gives us. Sometimes taking a few minutes to adjust our perspective can turn our everyday work into joy-filled worship again.

What My Heart Is Saying to You

Lord, you are good to me in ways beyond what I can even comprehend. Help me to consider your kindness and remember your benefits. I'm especially thankful for . . .

Amen.

What My Heart Is Hearing from You

Psalms 103–5

36

God Will Answer Your Desires with Good Things

Let them give thanks to the Lord for
his unfailing love
and his wonderful deeds for
mankind,
for he satisfies the thirsty
and fills the hungry with good things.

Psalm 107:8–9

My friend and I sit on a picnic blanket in the middle of a park. Moms with their children surround us. As we watch them, we both feel an ache, a hunger, an inner emptiness. Our friendship has been formed, in part, out of our common struggle with infertility. We talk about how hard it is to want something so badly and not get it.

Fast-forward five years. We're in a park again, but this time it's for her son's birthday party. As I watch the smile on her face, I think about how full her life seems. As she asks how I'm doing, I share about my latest book and the new opportunities God is giving me to bring life into the world through words. I tell her that in a totally different way, my life feels full and my desires satisfied.

God answered my friend and me in very different ways. He filled her baby-hungry heart with an actual, physical child. He did the same for me by making me a mother to the hearts of thousands of women, many of whom I will never meet until heaven. For both of us, the journey took years, tears, and a lot of unexpected twists and turns. But eventually we both realized that the ache we felt that first day in the park was gone.

God promises that he will satisfy the thirsty and fill the hungry with good things. He is not out to starve our souls. Yet sometimes what he places on our plates may not be what we wanted. So we turn our heads like toddlers and declare we will not eat our broccoli. Then we blame God when we walk away from the table still feeling hungry. Yet he knows to give us what we want—even if it seems to us like a very good thing—would actually not be what's best.

Deciding to "eat our broccoli" is an act of faith. It doesn't taste better when we put it in our mouths. It's not suddenly transformed into ice cream just because we've been obedient. It's often hard to swallow. But over time we begin to reap the benefits. We become healthier, stronger, and more whole.

Only God knows what our hearts truly need to eat. We can compare what's on our plates to that of those around us at the table and decide we got the bad end of the deal. Can't I just have what she's having? It's in those moments God asks us to trust that he knows what's good—what will truly satisfy our hunger and nourish us. When we do so, he promises to fill us up.

I'm so glad I didn't push away the plate God put in front of me. It wasn't easy. I had a lot of days when I wanted to throw the peas at the wall. I longed to pour hot fudge over everything and make it all better. I cried into my carrots. But now I wouldn't trade what God gave me for anything. Would I have chosen it for myself? Nope. But would I exchange it now if I could? Never.

I learned firsthand what this means: "Taste and see that the LORD is good" (Ps. 34:8).

When your heart is hungry, come to God's table. You're always welcome. And you'll always be served with love.

What My Heart Is Saying to You

Lord, you are the only One who truly knows what my heart needs. Help me be content with what you have for my life. Thank you for understanding how hard that can be sometimes. Right now I'm hungry for . . .

Amen.

What My Heart Is Hearing from You

Psalms 106–8

37

God Wants to Help When You Don't Know What to Do

The fear of the Lord is the beginning of
wisdom;
all who follow his precepts have good
understanding.
To him belongs eternal praise.

Psalm 111:10

A question comes up in the middle of the meeting. No one around the table is sure of the answer. In less than ten seconds, someone has whipped out a phone and said, "I'll look it up online." We all nod and wait for the response to our query to come streaming in from cyberspace. In our technological age, it seems many of us would tweak the beginning of the verse above, "Access to the internet is the beginning of wisdom." Now, I'm not knocking the search capabilities of our computers and phones. When it comes to information, the internet is a brilliant source.

Yet long before computers were even thought of, a greater source of wisdom existed. He spoke the world into being and hung the stars in place, and he has every hair on your head numbered. The only trouble seems to be that he tends to be a lot more vague than the search results on our screens. We want a recipe for chicken, and all we need to do is click Enter for five million results to appear. Then we pick one and we're ready for dinner. But when we want a recipe for life, the process isn't as clear. We can become frustrated when we confuse *knowledge* with *wisdom*. Knowledge is about information. Wisdom is about transformation.

Wisdom begins when we say, "I can find 684 ways to stain my back deck, but I can't figure out how to get this stain off my soul. God, will you help me?" In other words, we come to a place where we know we don't have all the answers that matter. When we do, God is ready and willing to help us. "If any of you lacks wisdom, you should ask God, who gives generously to all without finding fault, and it will be given to you" (James 1:5).

When we see the word *fear* in the psalm above, we can feel as if we should be afraid to come to God to ask for help. But this kind of fear is about awe and respect. It's recognizing God knows far more than we do and he alone is the source of what we need. The psalmist shares the progression that unfolds when we enter the process of truly seeking God:

> *Wisdom*—We go to God for help and insight with a specific situation.
>
> *Understanding*—We realize God truly knows what's best for us.
>
> *Praise*—We joyfully affirm that God is good and he has helped us.

Whatever is on your mind today, you can bring it to God. You can freely say to him, "I don't know what to do. Will you please help me?" He may answer in many different ways—through his Word, through other believers, or from an entirely unexpected source. It may seem as if your heart knows in an instant what to do, or it may take a long time for the solution to come. He might grant you what you ask or take you on an entirely different path. *But God will answer.* And when he does, you can trust it will be what your heart has truly been searching for all along.

What My Heart Is Saying to You

Lord, thank you for being the source of all wisdom. I'm glad I can come to you when I'm not sure what to do. I trust that you will hear my heart and be willing to answer. Please help me with . . .

Amen.

What My Heart Is Hearing from You

Psalms 109–11

38

God Will Be with You through the Whole Process

From the rising of the sun to the place
where it sets,
the name of the Lord is to be praised.

Psalm 113:3

I can hear the excitement in her voice. "I met someone," she gushes, "and I think he might be the one." A few weeks later, I ask her how it's going. "Great!" she replies. "We love being together." Then one day I get a tearful call. "We broke up," she sighs into the phone. "It's over." The sun rose, shone, and set on that relationship. What my friend did in each of those phases makes her remarkable. She found a way to see God in each one.

I've watched many of my other single friends do the same. I marvel at their ability to do so. I tend to be a "rising of the sun" praise giver. When something is brand-new, I'm excited. I can clearly see God's hand, and I'm willing to follow wherever he's going. Then high noon comes and I'm hot, tired, and ready to be done. The praise I offered when the day began can turn into discontent pretty quickly. And when the sun goes down on a dream in my life? I can get downright whiny.

God and I are working through this together. He's gently saying to my heart, "Holley, I'm equally present in all phases of the process. I'm there when you begin. I'm there in the difficult or glorious middle. I'm there when it comes to an end."

God wants me to praise him through the whole process because it affirms that though my circumstances may change, *who he is stays the same*. We desperately need to know this, especially when the relationship is unraveling, the dream is fading, or the world around us is growing darker.

Sometimes we can resent that God wants us to praise him all the time (or maybe that's just me).

But when he does so, he's actually doing something deeply loving for our hearts. We're human. We get scared. We don't like uncertainty. So by asking us to praise him even in our most difficult moments, God is creating a safe space for our hearts. He's reminding us that we are loved, we don't have to control everything, and he has a plan for our lives.

My friend went on to meet someone new, and she's now engaged. She told me, "I'm so glad I didn't stay in that other relationship! I felt devastated when it ended. But God had something so much better that I couldn't see yet. I'm grateful I didn't let my heart get bitter, or I wouldn't have been able to receive what he had for me."

Praise protects our hearts. It keeps us open to what God may have for us in the future. It prepares us to live another day—to watch the sun rise and set again. As long as we're on this earth, that's the cycle we live in. Beginnings and endings, starts and stops, light and darkness. Yet in all of those we can know that God is there, he cares, and he's going to make sure we have what we need for this day . . . every minute of it.

What My Heart Is Saying to You

Lord, you are my God from the rising of the sun to the setting of the same. Even in the hard moments, I choose to love and serve you. Nothing in my life is certain but you. Today I praise you for . . .

Amen.

What My Heart Is Hearing from You

Psalms 112–14

39

God Doesn't Expect You to Be "Fine"

I trusted in the Lord *when I said,*
"I am greatly afflicted."

Psalm 116:10

A friend and I swap stories over slices of pizza. We each share about seasons in our lives when we felt pressure to be "perfect." We both still struggle with that at times (doesn't every woman?), but God has brought us to new places of freedom. I ask her, "What was the turning point for you?" She describes one of the most difficult days of her life. She went to church that evening and someone asked, "How are you?" and she said, "I'm not okay." Being able to finally say that out loud changed her on the inside too. I instantly thought back to a similar moment in my life during a season full of sorrow. I showed up at small group and knew that if someone asked how I was doing, "Fine" would not be an option.

For years I'd believed that if I ever came to a place where I couldn't muster up the strength to just say "Fine," it would be a crisis of faith. But it turned out to be the opposite. When I could no longer keep up my façade, God could begin the real work of healing in my life. It turned out he was just waiting for me to say, "I'm not okay." That statement is actually much more powerful and faith-filled than "I'm fine." Admitting you're hurting requires courage and vulnerability.

When I read the psalm above, it stopped me in my tracks. I stared at the sentences and kept repeating them again and again in my mind. Something didn't seem right.

"I trusted in the LORD when I said, 'I am greatly afflicted.'"

I thought it should say instead, "I trusted in the LORD when I said, 'I'm doing great!'"

Yes, of course we can honor God by praising him in the happy times of our lives. But we also bring him glory by saying, "I'm having a really hard time right now." Coming to that place means we've stopped trying to protect ourselves. And that shows we believe we have a Protector. It means we have stopped trying to be perfect. And that reflects our belief that Someone loves us just as we are. It means we're admitting we don't know what the future will hold. But we're confident that there is One who will hold us no matter what happens.

I used to worry that if I didn't answer "Fine," I would make God look bad. But I realized that answering "Fine" actually says, "I'm too afraid to tell you the truth." When I say, "Not fine," I'm declaring, "I'm not afraid to tell you the truth, because I know Someone bigger and stronger than I am is going to take care of me."

Kids who have parents who love them are not afraid to cry over skinned knees. They're not hesitant to holler for help. They know they can always say, "I'm not okay!" because someone will come for them. If a child is afraid to show any pain or weakness, we wonder what's going on in their home.

You don't have to be as strong as you think you do. You don't have to pretend. You don't have to put up a good front for God. He can handle where your heart really is today. You can tell him the truth. He already knows anyway. He also knows you love and trust him. And when you say, “I’m not fine today,” it’s just another way you show that’s true.

What My Heart Is Saying to You

Lord, it’s wonderful to me that I can be honest with you. I’m not “fine” today, and there are some things I want to share with you because I love and trust you . . .

Amen.

What My Heart Is Hearing from You

Psalms 115–17

40

God Can Free You from Life's Pressure

When hard pressed, I cried to the LORD;
he brought me into a spacious place.

Psalm 118:5

She opens her eyes to a new day and stumbles into the kitchen for her first cup of coffee. On the way, she pauses to look at the calendar on the refrigerator. Her schedule is full from morning to night. She sighs and sits down with her mug to check her bank account through her phone. The numbers reveal it's almost empty. "When did my life stop having any room to breathe?" she wonders.

But just as quickly as the thought comes, she pushes it away. She tells herself instead, "I shouldn't think that way. Look how blessed I am! The activities on my calendar represent people I love and opportunities I've been given. The bank account pays for the lifestyle I have. I need to just stop complaining and be grateful." Yet as she gets up from the table, the lingering feeling that something isn't quite right remains.

We're not made to live under continual pressure. Our culture tries to tell us otherwise. We're supposed to pursue success, keep a busy social calendar, and have all the latest and greatest products on the market. We're told that's what leads to happiness. Yet we end up feeling behind most of the time. Or if we do manage to keep up, we discover those promises from the commercials simply don't deliver. We can even turn our faith into a part of the pressure we feel. We have to be at church every time the doors are open, pray more, and try harder.

But eventually something happens. Either we explode or we become completely deflated. We've all watched the lives of prominent leaders break into little pieces right before our eyes. Or we've known someone who used to live with joy and passion but now struggles to get out of bed each day. Here's a reality of the universe whether we're talking about inanimate objects or our hearts: ongoing pressure simply isn't sustainable.

The day we realize we just can't do it all can feel like our biggest moment of failure. But it's actually the first step to true success. Saying "Enough!" isn't a word of weakness. It's one of the most powerful ones you can utter. It means that you believe God has a better way. It means you're not trying to gain the approval of others but rather you've decided to live for the joy of your Master. It means you believe who the Creator made you is good and your identity is secure in him.

One of the only other places in Scripture where the phrase "hard pressed" is found comes from the apostle Paul:

> But we have this treasure in jars of clay to show that this all-surpassing power is from God and not from us. We are hard pressed on every side, but not crushed; perplexed, but not in despair; persecuted, but not abandoned; struck down, but not destroyed. (2 Cor. 4:7–9)

God's power replaces the pressure. Sometimes God takes us to a new place, and sometimes he makes new space inside us. A new space of freedom and peace with plenty of room for joy. The process of changing our lives will vary with each of us. For some, it may mean saying a difficult no to some worthwhile things on our calendars. For others it may mean introducing healthier habits like exercise to deal with stress. It might mean a few tweaks or a transformation. Only God knows what you need. Whatever it looks like for you, God will give you the power to do it. Over time you'll find that instead of the world pushing in, you'll be living from a new space of strength and resilience deep within.

What My Heart Is Saying to You

Lord, sometimes my life can feel so full of pressure. I pray you would replace that with your power. Please bring me into a spacious place and make more room in my life for . . .

Amen.

What My Heart Is Hearing from You

Psalms 118, 120

Because of its length, Psalm 119 is separate.

41

God's Ways Are Best for You

My soul is weary with sorrow;
strengthen me according to your word.
Keep me from deceitful ways;
be gracious to me and teach me your law.

Psalm 119:28–29

It's been a long day, and I find myself standing in front of the kitchen cabinet. I reach for a bar of chocolate and carry it with me to the couch. I flip through the channels until I find a show that promises to provide an escape. During commercials, I complain to my husband about everything that has gone wrong recently. By the end of the night, I expect to feel better. I've done everything this world tells us to do, right? Give yourself a treat. Get some time to relax. Go ahead and vent. But as I lay my head on the pillow, my heart is even heavier than before. "Why didn't you help me?" I ask Jesus. And it seems he replies, "You didn't ask."

Huh.

Now, there's nothing wrong with the occasional chocolate, relaxing TV show, or sharing your feelings with someone you trust. But I wasn't using those gifts in the ways God intended. I was turning to them as a substitute for what I really needed instead. I needed truth, not a snack. I needed rest, not a fantasy. I needed encouragement, not a gripe session. A lot of the time we don't do what's really best for us. As humans we can tend to reach for the easiest thing rather than what will truly restore our souls.

That's why the psalmist says, "My soul is weary with sorrow; strengthen me *according to your word*. Keep me from *deceitful ways*." He's saying, "God, I know that I can fool myself about what I really need. Please comfort me in the ways you intend. Keep me from sabotaging my life without even realizing it."

Some people can take passages like this to the extreme and say, "See, you can't trust your heart." Then they point to Scriptures like, "The heart is deceitful above all things and beyond cure. Who can understand it?" (Jer. 17:9). But the verse following that one says God knows our hearts. And even more than that, when we come to know Jesus, he gives us a brand-new heart. Verses like Jeremiah 17:9 are talking about unredeemed hearts. So, yes, you can trust your heart because the Holy Spirit now lives within you.

But there is a part of you that still can't be trusted, and that's your flesh. As long as you live, it will try to persuade you that the ways of the world are better than God's. That's where we need help in hard times. Because when life gets tough, our flesh starts hollering the loudest. But ultimately it has been crucified with Christ and has no power over us. So we can pray, "God, keep me aligned with your way of doing life. Show me when my flesh is trying to trick me into settling for less than your best. Protect me and help me listen to your voice above all others. Strengthen me according to your Word and keep me from deceitful ways. Now I'm going to put down the cookie and call an encouraging friend instead. Amen."

What My Heart Is Saying to You

Lord, you understand my heart and you know what I truly need. Help me to listen to your voice. Comfort me and give me strength according to your Word. One truth I want to hold on to today is . . .

Amen.

What My Heart Is Hearing from You

Psalm 119:1–88

42

God Isn't Done with Your Story Yet

Streams of tears flow from my eyes,
for your law is not obeyed.

Psalm 119:136

I glance at my counseling schedule and see it's a full afternoon. My first client is recovering from childhood abuse. My second is reeling after learning her husband is having an affair. The next one mourns over a prodigal child. So many stories, so much hurt. Each of these situations reminds me of what a leader taught me to say in a grief support group: "I'm so sorry. It's not supposed to be this way."

Pain wasn't ever a part of God's plan for your life. And all hurt can ultimately be traced back in some way to sin, whether that's a specific action by an individual or simply the reality that we're living in a broken world. Sin always brings death in some way. It might be the death of innocence, a marriage, or a life. We were never meant to deal with any of these. We were created for life, abundance, and joy. God is still committed to restoring those to us. It will just take until heaven for the process to be complete.

In the meantime, we can know that God aches with us over the state of this world. He recognizes that what we're facing isn't the way it's supposed to be. Jesus stood outside the tomb of his friend Lazarus and wept, even though he knew in just a few moments he would raise Lazarus from the dead. I believe those tears came because he hates sin and death too. He doesn't like to see his children hurting. When we believe God wants us to be in pain, we deeply misunderstand his heart.

When he arrived, Martha and Mary both said the same words to him:

> "Lord," Martha said to Jesus, "if you had been here, my brother would not have died." (John 11:21)

Mary . . . said, "Lord, if you had been here, my brother would not have died." (John 11:32)

We know these two women from the famous story where Martha is working hard to serve Jesus while Mary sits at his feet. They clearly approached life very differently, and yet death evoked the same response in them. It's the same one we usually feel too. A part of us wonders, "God, where were you? Why didn't you stop this from happening?"

Jesus doesn't answer this question directly for Martha or Mary. Instead he mourns with them and then brings new life. That's the same process he still engages in with us now. Most of the time we won't know why we're facing the challenges that we are. But we can know God hurts with us. And he does promise that death is never, ever the end. Whether it's a relationship, job, or dream that has died, God always finds a way to bring new life. If you're asking God, "Where are you today?" he's answering, "I'm here with you. I know this is not the way it's supposed to be. My heart hurts with yours. I'm going to make this right."

Sometimes the resurrection happens sooner than we think it will (like with Lazarus), sometimes we wait (like with Jesus), and sometimes it's not until eternity.

But it will come. No matter what page your story is on right now, this is not the end. With God there is only one ending—and it's actually a beginning.

> "God's dwelling place is now among the people, and he will dwell with them. They will be his people, and God himself will be with them and be their God. He will wipe every tear from their eyes. There will be no more death or mourning or crying or pain, for the old order of things has passed away." He who was seated on the throne said, "I am making everything new!" (Rev. 21:3–5)

What My Heart Is Saying to You

Lord, this world is not as it should be. It brings me comfort to know you understand that. You are a God of restoration and resurrection. Please bring new life to . . .

Amen.

What My Heart Is Hearing from You

Psalm 119:89–176

43

God Is Not Tired of You

He who watches over you will not slumber;
indeed, he who watches over Israel
will neither slumber nor sleep.

Psalm 121:3–4

Confession: New Year's Eve has become a bit of a challenge. I can remember easily staying awake until midnight all through my teenage years. Sometimes my friends and I would even watch the night turn into dawn before crashing, still in our clothes, to sleep most of the day away. But now I find myself yawning a bit earlier, downing a little more caffeine, hearing the call of my pillow quite intensely. Even when I *want* to stay awake, I can only fight the urge for so long.

It turns out I'm not alone in the need for sleep. Humans can't get by without it. When researchers deprive study participants of sleep for long periods of time, they note significant drops in levels of functioning as well as bizarre behavior. We're simply not wired to live tired.

While Jesus spent time on earth, he grew weary at times too. We hear about him resting after a long walk and napping in a boat, for example. *So being tired isn't sinful.* If it were, Jesus wouldn't have needed rest or sleep. But being tired *is* distinctly human rather than divine.

God doesn't sleep. Not a wink. While you're safely dreaming, he's watching over you. While you're going about your day, he sees every detail. He never needs to lean back in his chair to shut his eyes for a moment. He doesn't nod off in meetings. He won't miss your call for help because he's snoozing on the sofa.

Not only does God not sleep, he doesn't even get tired. He always has enough energy to engage with you. He always has enough time to listen to your heart. He always has the power to meet your needs.

It doesn't matter what time of the day or night it may be—God is ready to respond.

With the people we love, we're careful not to ask too much of them. We don't want to wear them out or use up a disproportionate amount of the energy or time they have in their day. But you don't have to be concerned about that with God. His personal resources are infinite.

God is not tired. *And he is not tired of you.* No matter how many times you've brought the same request to him. No matter how often you've asked for help with the same struggle. No matter how frequently you've needed to just sit and cry with him. He can handle all of it. You are not too much for God.

Not only that, he *wants* to be there for you. He's not responding to you because he has to—he's doing so because he loves you. His love is not one of obligation. It's a love of choice. He chose you. He delights in you. He invites you to come to him. Anytime. Anyplace. All 365 days a year.

What My Heart Is Saying to You

Lord, it's such a relief to realize you never grow tired. You always have enough time and energy for me. I can't reduce you or drain you in any way. So I'm freely coming to you to share this today . . .

Amen.

What My Heart Is Hearing from You

Psalms 121–23

44

God Gives You Permission to Laugh

When the L*ORD restored the fortunes*
of Zion,
we were like those who dreamed.
Our mouths were filled with laughter,
our tongues with songs of joy.
Then it was said among the nations,
"The L*ORD has done great things*
for them."

Psalm 126:1–2

I'm seated at a table with family and friends of those who have lost loved ones. Our time together has been somber so far, and then laughter bursts through the pain. Immediately the source of the laugh apologizes. "I'm so sorry," she says. "We were just talking about a funny memory. I know it's not respectful to laugh right now." I look at her and gently say, "Laughter is a gift from God to help us through the grief. It's okay to laugh—at times like these it can even be a bit like worship. Because it says to the world, 'Even when things are this hard, I still have hope somewhere deep inside.'"

Over the coming weeks as hearts continue to heal, laughter becomes even more common in this group. We discover it is indeed "good medicine" for grief (Prov. 17:22). When we have many hard days in a row, we can begin to feel as if we don't have the right to laugh or feel joy anymore. That can especially be true if our trouble affects someone else too. Who are we to laugh when our spouse has cancer, when our friend's child has died, when the company just laid off our co-workers? But laughing in those times, when it's done with sensitivity and grace, can help sustain us as well as others who are hurting too.

Laughter reminds us that we are not our circumstances.

It gives us a glimpse of a better future ahead.

It builds resilience—it's like exercise for our souls.

Laughter also tells the world that God has been good to us. And there is no time that's more powerful than when our circumstances seem to be truly bad. Does this mean we need to force cheerfulness when our hearts are breaking? Not at all. Honest grief gives God glory too. Like we talked about before, it shows we trust him with our pain. We just don't have to feel limited to always staying in sorrow. Lighter moments can help so much with heavy burdens.

Our bodies literally release feel-good chemicals when we laugh. God has designed you to benefit from giggles as well as tears. Both help us in hard times. Some of my favorite moments with people I love have started with tears of sadness and ended in tears of joy. There's something healing about experiencing the whole range of emotions together. "There is a time for everything . . . a time to weep and a time to laugh" (Eccl. 3:1, 4). Whichever you need today, it's okay.

What My Heart Is Saying to You

Lord, thank you for the gifts of tears *and* laughter. You have given us so many ways to express our emotions. A memory that always makes me laugh is . . .

Amen.

What My Heart Is Hearing from You

Psalms 124–26

45

God Can Fill In the Gaps for You

In vain you rise early
and stay up late,
toiling for food to eat—
for he grants sleep to those he loves.

Psalm 127:2

"I feel like I can't keep up," she says as we talk about how she's managing work, family, and other responsibilities in the middle of a difficult season. "I try my best not to fall behind, but it takes a toll on me—physically, emotionally, and even spiritually. What should I do?" I gently smile and reply, "Go home and take a nap."

When hard days come, we tend to carry on with life as usual. We put on a brave face and continue trying to make it to every event on our calendars and check off all the items on our to-do list. We may even increase what we're doing in an effort to make things better. Yet over time we find our energy and joy draining away.

It's okay to cut back sometimes. It's all right to say, "At another time I would love to do that, but I simply can't right now." It's allowable to admit, "I really need some extra rest right now." You're not a human treadmill, and you can't sustain the same pace all the time. That's simply not how we're created.

When we think about pulling back or slowing down, instantly we can feel the fear. What will happen? The answer: whatever needs to happen. Because God will fill in the gaps for what you lack right now. Jesus turned a few fish and loaves of bread into a meal for thousands. He can turn whatever you have to offer into enough too.

Sometimes we need to step back to realize, in the best possible way, that the world doesn't rely on us as much as we think. Everything can go on just fine without us for a bit. Here's the catch: we'll never know that unless we take time off now and then. It does our hearts good to have a little "reality check" once in a while. When we rest, we're reminded that we're not God.

At a minimum, we each need a weekly Sabbath—especially when we're facing a challenging situation in our lives. God gave us the Sabbath as a gift. It's a time for our bodies, hearts, and minds to be restored. Because we're people of grace, it isn't about keeping a law but instead receiving what we need. And that looks different for each one of us. I practice a weekly "cyber Sabbath" when I unplug from everything electronic for one twenty-four-hour period. You might have a physical job, and in that case you might sit down and plug in for the same amount of time. Ask God what you need on that day to be restored.

The other days we can live with a Sabbath heart as well. That means knowing we're not responsible for the universe. It's believing God can turn whatever we have to give into what's needed—even if we believe we should be able to do more. It's trusting that we are not on this earth for striving and work but for worship.

You have permission to slow down, do less, and rest more today.

What My Heart Is Saying to You

Lord, thank you for granting sleep to those you love. Help me to see rest the way you do. Give me the courage to do less and trust more. Today I will not . . .

Amen.

What My Heart Is Hearing from You

Psalms 127–29

46

God Isn't Holding Anything against You

If you, Lord, kept a record of sins,
Lord, who could stand?
But with you there is forgiveness,
so that we can, with reverence,
serve you.

Psalm 130:3–4

I step up to the library counter with a stack of books in my hand. The librarian, who happens to be wearing a name tag that says "Bunny," scans my card and then looks at the computer. "Oh my!" she declares. "You have a fine." She narrows her eyes and slides her glasses down her nose. "You simply must learn to turn your books in on time." I stare back at her, completely intimidated by the gray-haired Bunny in front of me, and manage to stammer, "Yes ma'am." She hands me my books carefully, as if she's not sure I should be trusted with any more of the library's treasure. I bolt out the door before she decides to take any of them back.

When we come to God with requests, we can picture the exchange going much the same way mine did with Bunny the librarian. We step up to the counter of heaven with a stack of hopes. God scans our hearts and declares, "Oh my! You've got quite the list of sins here." We picture him reviewing our wrongdoings before deciding if we can indeed be trusted with what we've asked for this time. We might even feel as if he's waving us away. "Go pay your dues and then try again."

But God keeps no record of wrongs. He doesn't have a file with your past in it. He's not racking up fines for you to pay when you get to the gates of glory. In youth group years ago, the leaders used to scare us silly by saying that when we got to heaven a giant movie would play all of our sins for everyone to see. You can imagine how that terrified teenagers. Yet at the same time, it often did little to change our ways. Fear may last for a moment, but it's not enough to transform our hearts. And the "heavenly horror film" scenario simply isn't true. We're changed by love, not the law. And at the center of love is forgiveness.

When we deeply, truly believe we're forgiven, then we begin to respond from a new place. We have appreciation for the One who has canceled our debts, and we long to serve out of joy. So if you've been worried that the hard times you're facing are simply because you "have to pay your dues," then you can let that fear go. God doesn't work that way with us. When he forgives us, he means it. We may face natural consequences, of course. For example, if you drink on the job and get fired, then you're going to experience the pain of being without employment. But God is not saying, "Oh, you're asking me for a blessing today? Well, I'd love to give that to you, but it looks like you still need to pay for something you did back in 1982." What's done is done.

Today we truly can "approach God's throne of grace with confidence, so that we may receive mercy and find grace to help us in our time of need" (Heb. 4:16). Bunny the librarian might be out to get you, but your Savior is always willing to give you grace.

What My Heart Is Saying to You

Lord, your forgiveness is more than I can comprehend or ever deserve. I'm so glad you keep no record of wrongs. Instead you want to give me grace and bless my life. I'm coming to you with confidence to ask for . . .

Amen.

What My Heart Is Hearing from You

Psalms 130–32

47

God Will Use You to Help Others

Praise the Lord, *all you servants of the*
Lord
who minister by night in the house of
the Lord.
Lift up your hands in the sanctuary
and praise the Lord.
May the Lord *bless you from Zion,*
he who is the Maker of heaven and
earth.

Psalm 134

My husband and I sit with our eyes glued to the television. A tornado has ripped through a town only a few hours away from us. Scenes of destruction flash across the screen as survivors tell their heartbreaking stories. The news anchor points to the rubble behind her and says, "The rescue workers are here and they will work through the night." As I drift off to sleep later, I pray for those who are still laboring in the darkness on behalf of those who need them desperately.

If you've been through difficulties in life, then you may be called to help others in similar ways. I love how the psalm above says there are those who "minister by night in the house of the LORD." This entire psalm seems to be dedicated to these people. It's one of the shortest psalms in the entire book and contains only these three verses. Again, this seems to indicate those who minister in the night have a special calling.

I've known women like this, and they always amaze me. Pam Long is a grief support leader who gives healing hugs and wise words to those who have lost loved ones. My friend Jenni Saake helps those with infertility and chronic illness to find encouragement and new strength. Fellow writer Sarah Markley goes to the hard places in marriage with those who are hurting. All of these women have this in common: they have faced similar struggles to the ones in the lives of those they are helping. God has brought these women through the night, and they have willingly chosen to go back into places of darkness with others. Is there anything more courageous?

Perhaps you are one of those women who is helping others as well. You may not even have realized it yet. You could simply find yourself placing your hand on the shoulder of a woman who's hurting in church on Sunday. You might realize your phone is ringing a little more often with those who need a comforting word or prayer. Maybe in your workplace your office is the place people step into and close the door behind them so they can share what's really happening. If you are coming alongside those who are in pain in any way, then you are "ministering in the night." Thank you.

Your life is a powerful way that God is bringing light into many dark places. You shine brighter than you know. You make a difference.

By dawn the next morning, the rescue workers had found more people alive in the rubble. One described hearing a call for help and then extending a hand to pull a woman to safety. That might be you today. It may be your moment to hear a voice in the night, reach out, and touch a life. Don't be afraid of the darkness. God will light the way for you.

> If I say, "Surely the darkness will hide me
> and the light become night around me,"
> even the darkness will not be dark to you;
> the night will shine like the day,
> for darkness is as light to you.
> (Ps. 139:11–12)

What My Heart Is Saying to You

Lord, you have been with me through all the nights in my life. I pray that you will use me to bring comfort to others as well. Show me how I can bring light to those around me. Someone who is especially on my heart today is . . .

Amen.

What My Heart Is Hearing from You

Psalms 133–35

48

God Has Words for Your Heart to Hold On To

Give thanks to the Lord, for he is good.
His love endures forever.
Give thanks to the God of gods.
His love endures forever.
Give thanks to the Lord of lords:
His love endures forever.

Psalm 136:1–3

Around the start of each year, it seems blogs begin filling with women who are choosing a word to focus on for the next twelve months. For some it's *joy*. Others pick *courage*. And many emphasize *gratitude*. Over the coming weeks, it's interesting to see how these words influence their responses to various circumstances. I watch these women use phrases like, "Even though this is happening, I'm still finding the joy" or "I'm learning to be braver through what I'm facing right now."

It seems the psalmist above had a similar tactic. If he had chosen a word, it would probably have been *love*. The phrase "His love endures forever" appears twenty-six times in this one psalm. He describes all kinds of circumstances the Israelites have faced. Some challenging and others joyful. After each one, he reaffirms the love of God. The chosen people of Israel have been through many changes, and yet this one thing remains the same: *his love endures forever*.

Our hearts need truth we can return to again and again as well. When we know the truth, we can build our lives on it. As Jesus said:

> Therefore everyone who hears these words of mine and puts them into practice is like a wise man who built his house on the rock. The rain came down, the streams rose, and the winds blew and beat against that house; yet it did not fall, because it had its foundation on the rock. But everyone who hears these words of mine and does not put them into practice is

> like a foolish man who built his house on sand. The rain came down, the streams rose, and the winds blew and beat against that house, and it fell with a great crash. (Matt. 7:24–27)

While the truths of Scripture apply to all of us as believers, it seems there are particular ones we each personally need more at certain times. Like the women choosing a specific word at the start of the year or the psalmist repeating the phrase, "His love endures forever," those truths can add stability in the shaky circumstances we're experiencing. They can also influence our actions. When we find ourselves unsure of what to do or how to respond, they give us a place to go back to where we can stand firm.

The specific truth we need for a certain time in our lives often starts with a whisper in our hearts. Then God reveals it in other ways too—through his Word, wise friends, and even unexpected avenues. Our part is primarily to keep our ears and hearts open to receive what he has for us. Then we build on it by living it out. What truth keeps coming back to your mind and heart? Turn it into part of the foundation for your life that will give you a firm place to stand no matter what happens.

What My Heart Is Saying to You

Lord, thank you for giving me truth to build my life on so I can be secure. Help me to hear what you're saying to me, and show me how I can apply it. A word or phrase that I feel drawn to focus on is . . .

Amen.

What My Heart Is Hearing from You

Psalms 136–38

49

God Hears What Your Heart Has to Say

Before a word is on my tongue
you, Lord, know it completely.

Psalm 139:4

I had a great-aunt and great-uncle who were married for almost seventy years. Through decades of sharing life, they developed a language all their own. They could finish each other's sentences and speak volumes with just a look, and they used phrases with meanings only known to the two of them. Intimacy and familiarity helped them know each other far beyond just what sounds and syllables could communicate. When you know someone's heart, you don't need much of an explanation.

God also knows what we're going to say even before we do because he knows our hearts. "The mouth speaks what the heart is full of" (Matt. 12:34). Even before you pause to pray, God already knows what you're going to say. He can finish your sentences because he's heard them being formed deep within you. That means prayer is not about information—it's about intimacy. It builds our relationship with God when we speak to him and listen for his response.

Yet because God knows us so completely, we also don't have to feel pressure to have just the right words. We've all heard fancy prayers that make us wonder if we should ever dare to speak to Jesus again. But what matters to him is not our language but the meaning behind it. "Help me, Jesus" is one of the most powerful, pleasing prayers you can ever say. So when you're struggling, it's okay if you're not sure how to express what you're feeling to God. You can simply tell him, "You know my heart. You know what I need. I love and trust you. Please do what is best."

We can also rest in knowing that Jesus and the Holy Spirit add to our prayers:

> Christ Jesus who died—more than that, who was raised to life—is at the right hand of God and is also interceding for us. (Rom. 8:34)

> In the same way, the Spirit helps us in our weakness. We do not know what we ought to pray for, but the Spirit himself intercedes for us through wordless groans. And he who searches our hearts knows the mind of the Spirit, because the Spirit intercedes for God's people in accordance with the will of God. (Rom. 8:26–27)

Because of that, we don't have to feel pressure to have enough words or even the right ones. Jesus and the Spirit intercede on our behalf according to God's will. So whatever we ask for, they can translate it into what we truly need. God knows we don't have the same perspective he does. He understands we don't have the wisdom of eternity. He remembers that we are finite, limited beings. So you don't have to fear getting in trouble for asking for the "wrong thing" when you pray. Just be honest, surrender your will, and then ask Jesus and the Spirit to intercede for you.

A loving marriage that lasts for a lifetime is a haven for our hearts. Prayer is meant to be one too. God's presence is a place you can always come to and trust you'll be accepted, cherished, and fully known in a way that's beyond words.

What My Heart Is Saying to You

Lord, it's a beautiful gift to be able to connect with you through prayer. You know my heart and all that I long to say, including . . .

Amen.

What My Heart Is Hearing from You

Psalms 139–41

50

God Will Train You to Do Battle

Praise be to the LORD my Rock,
who trains my hands for war,
my fingers for battle.
He is my loving God and my fortress,
my stronghold and my deliverer,
my shield, in whom I take refuge.

Psalm 144:1–2

We're talking about the battles we face in daily life. One woman says, "I think we just have to fight the enemy. We need to step out in faith and knock him down with the truth." Another says, "I believe God is our protector and he's the One who defends us. I ask him for protection every day." They turn to me and ask, "Which approach do you think we're supposed to take?" I smile and answer, "Both."

There seems to be a paradox in the psalm above. David says God "trains my hands for war" and then adds that God is "my stronghold and my deliverer." How do those two fit together? It seems there are times when God asks us to go to the front lines. What David recognizes is that God never sends us into those situations unprepared. He teaches us what we need to know for victory. He also equips us with armor to protect us:

> Be strong in the Lord and in his mighty power. Put on the full armor of God, so that you can take your stand against the devil's schemes. For our struggle is not against flesh and blood, but against the rulers, against the authorities, against the powers of this dark world and against the spiritual forces of evil in the heavenly realms. Therefore put on the full armor of God, so that when the day of evil comes, you may be able to stand your ground, and after you have done everything, to stand. (Eph. 6:10–13)

There are other times when God knows we're too weary or wounded to go to battle. When we can't fight, he does so on our behalf. "The LORD will fight for you; you need only to be still" (Exod. 14:14). He's not going to send you into a situation where you can't win.

We can ask God, "Please show me whether this is a time to fight or a time to be still." He will reveal what we need to do. Most of us naturally lean toward one approach or the other. That's because we're wired with a fight-or-flight system and have a preference for one. Think of a time when you were startled. Was your first reaction to throw a punch or jump under the table? If you came out swinging, you're probably a "fight" kind of girl. If you took cover, you're more likely to be someone who leans toward "flight." Both responses can be helpful, and neither one is better or worse than the other. We just need to know which one we automatically go to so we can make sure that's really what's best.

In most situations we don't have to react immediately, so take a moment to pause and pray. You can say to God, "I know you have promised me victory. Please show me the way you want that to happen.

Give me courage if it's time to fight, and give me patience if it's time to wait for you to act on my behalf." He'll show you what to do, and he'll be with you through the battle. You're already more than a conqueror, and you can never lose with God on your side.

What My Heart Is Saying to You

Lord, you are the One who gives me victory. You train me for war, and you also hide me away at times. Give me wisdom to know which one is best today as I face the battle of . . .

Amen.

What My Heart Is Hearing from You

Psalms 142–44

51

God Doesn't Want You to Stay Broken

He heals the brokenhearted
and binds up their wounds.

Psalm 147:3

As I drive down the highway, a truck pulls in front of me. I begin to switch lanes, and a rock pops up from the road and crashes against my windshield. Instantly a star-shaped crack appears. I call my husband and ask if I can stop by his office to show it to him. He observes the damage and then says, "Insurance probably won't fix it yet because it's not in your line of sight." We decide to watch the spot and see what happens. I don't look directly at it when I drive, but every once in a while I still catch a glimpse of it out of the corner of my eye. It may not be an immediate danger to me, but I still don't like that it's broken. "I can live with it a little longer," I tell myself.

We all have times when life comes flying at us fast. We're going along and our hearts get hit. Sometimes our whole world is instantly shattered. In those instances, it's easy to believe God will quickly come to our rescue. Many people describe sensing his presence nearer than ever before in times of trouble. But what about the times when it's not a boulder that comes into our world but instead a pebble? A part of us is broken, but it doesn't seem that bad. "I can keep going," we tell ourselves.

But God doesn't want us to stay broken in any area of our lives. He's not an insurance adjuster holding out until the last minute before he's willing to repair the damage. He wants us to be whole. He wants to heal our hearts. He wants to restore what has been damaged. We can come to him and say, "I'm tempted to believe this is small and I shouldn't even bother you with it. But I can see this hurt is there and I need your help." He's ready and willing to answer.

If we don't ask for him to repair our souls as we go, we can find ourselves full of broken spots. Or what starts as a crack in a corner of our lives can spread. Before we know it, we're unable to move forward. We don't have to let that happen. Every time we have a hard day, we can stop and say, "Ouch. Lord, please heal my broken heart and bind up this wound."

On our journey together you've been learning to live in new ways. I hope you're discovering it's okay to go to God as often as needed. It's okay to share your feelings with him. It's okay to stop trying so hard and lean on his grace instead.

I pray our time together has been part of the healing process for you. Keep pursuing more wholeness in your life in whatever ways you need. Seek out more resources, see a counselor, or confide in a trusted friend. When you say, "I will not live with ongoing brokenness," it's not an admission of weakness. It's an act of great courage. I'm cheering for you as you keep moving forward. There's so much good ahead for you. Don't let anything block your vision or get in your way. You've come so far already, my friend.

What My Heart Is Saying to You

Lord, you are the God who sees every part of me. You know the broken places in my life, and you want to make them whole again. Thank you for healing this part of my heart . . .

Amen.

What My Heart Is Hearing from You

Psalms 145–47

52

God Deserves Your Praise Forever

Let everything that has breath praise
the LORD.
Praise the LORD.

Psalm 150:6

It's not about you.

It's not about me.

It's about God.

When our world doesn't make sense and hard days come, that truth can set our hearts free. As long as we believe it's about us, we carry the weight of making everything okay. If it's about us, then there's no room for mistakes. If it's about us, then this life is all there is and our stories don't have a happy ending.

But it's not about us. It's about a God who loved us so much that he sent his Son to die on our behalf. It's about a God who greets us with a sunrise every morning and watches over us as we fall asleep every night. It's about a God who can see all of eternity and has promised us that we will be with him forever.

The verse above is the final one in Psalms. It seems fitting that the close to this beloved book of the Bible is a simple phrase: praise the Lord.

It's the one phrase we can always go back to, no matter what.

When we are tired, *praise the Lord.*

When we're not sure what's going to happen, *praise the Lord.*

When we're celebrating, *praise the Lord.*

Is this easy? Nope. Not in this world. Perhaps that's why the writer of Hebrews calls it "a sacrifice of praise" (Heb. 13:15). Choosing to see God's goodness in all the moments of our lives does feel like a sacrifice at times. And yet it's actually a gift God wants to offer us. He doesn't need our praise.

He doesn't suffer from low self-esteem. He doesn't have an ego that's too big. God loves us deeply and knows us intimately. He understands we're made for worship. We're designed to live in a way that's not about us. We're created to connect with a greater plan and purpose.

Hard days can make us forget who God is and who we are. Praise reminds us. It brings us home to the place where our hearts can heal and find joy. It replaces the lies we hear with the truth we need. It lifts our hands and helps us lay down our burdens.

In the introduction, I talked about how we were coming to a table to "taste and see that the LORD is good" (Ps. 34:8). I pray you're finishing our time together with a heart that's full. And like after any satisfying meal, it's time to thank the One who provided it for us.

Let's praise God together.

On the happy days.

On the hard days.

Today. Tomorrow. Forever.

Amen, my friend!

What My Heart Is Saying to You

Lord, thank you for filling my heart. This life is not about me. It's about you. I give you all I have and all I am. You are my God, and I belong to you forever. I praise you for . . .

Amen.

What My Heart Is Hearing from You

Psalms 148–50

Acknowledgments

Thanks to my fabulous team at Revell for all you do. You're more than my publisher. You're partners and friends. I'm especially grateful for my editorial and marketing girls—Jennifer Leep, Michele Misiak, Robin Barnett, Twila Bennett, and Wendy Wetzel.

Thanks to my strong and wise husband, Mark, who has his feet on the ground so I can keep my head in the clouds and my fingers on the keyboard. I love you.

To the encouraging friends in my real life and online, you are a gift, and I wouldn't be able to do this without you. Thank you for cheering me on and for being women of grace who teach me new things every day.

Most of all, to the One who walks with me through the hard days—thank you for letting me write with and for you. I'm your servant; may it be to me as you have said. Use me as little or as much as you want. And may my life bring you great joy.

Notes

Chapter 12 God Enjoys Your Joy

1. Gary Thomas, *Pure Pleasure: Why Do Christians Feel So Bad about Feeling Good?* (Grand Rapids: Zondervan, 2009), 17.

Chapter 17 God Is Speaking to You Today

1. Shauna Niequist, *Bittersweet: Thoughts on Change, Grace, and Learning the Hard Way* (Grand Rapids: Zondervan, 2010), 111–12.

Chapter 18 God Can Keep You Unharmed

1. Henry Cloud, *Necessary Endings: The Employees, Businesses, and Relationships That All of Us Have to Give Up in Order to Move Forward* (Grand Rapids: Zondervan, 2011), 21.

Chapter 23 God Will Bear Your Burdens

1. Paula Rinehart, *Strong Women, Soft Hearts: A Woman's Guide to Cultivating a Wise Heart and a Passionate Life* (Nashville: Thomas Nelson, 2001), 153.

About Holley

Holley Gerth is a bestselling writer, speaker, and life coach who loves sharing God's heart for women through words. She's done so through several books, a partnership with DaySpring, and her popular blog. Holley is also a cofounder of (in)courage, a website for women that received almost a million page views in its first six months.

Holley shares her heart and home with her husband, Mark. She lives in the South, likes to say "y'all," and would love to have coffee with you so she could hear all about you too. Until then, she hopes you'll hang out with her online at www.holleygerth.com.

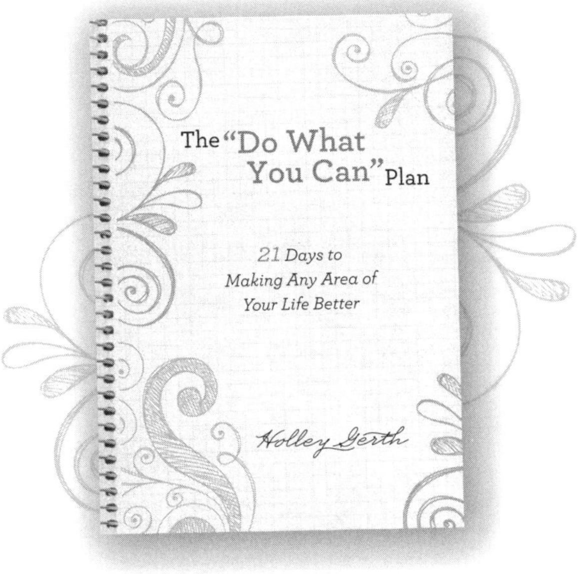